THE SECRET
SEDUCTRESS

Breaking the Destructive Cycle of
PORNOGRAPHY

PickingUp
ThePieces

DR. MARK LAASER & MICHAEL CHRISTIAN

The Secret Seductress: Breaking the Destructive Cycle of Pornography
© 2007 Mark Lasser

Published by Serendipity House Publishers
Nashville, Tennessee

ISBN: 1-5749-4223-9

Dewey Decimal Classification: 363.4
Subject Headings: PORNOGRAPHY \ SEXUAL DISORDERS

Scripture quotations marked HCSB taken from the *Holman Christian Standard Bible*®, Copyright © 1999, 2000, 2002, 2003 by Holman Bible Publishers. Used by permission.

Scriptures marked NASB from the *New American Standard Bible*®, © 1960, 1962, 1963, 1968, 1971, 1972, 1973, 1975, 1977, 1995 by the Lockman Foundation. Used by permission.

Scriptures marked NIV taken from the *Holy Bible, New International Version,* Copyright © 1973, 1978, 1984 by International Bible Society. Used by permission.

Scriptures marked The Message taken from the *THE MESSAGE,* Copyright © 1993, 1994, 1995, 1996, 2000, 2001, 2002. Used by permission of NavPress Publishing Group.

Scriptures marked NLT taken from the *The Holy Bible, New Living Translation,* Copyright © 1996. Used by permission of Tyndale House Publishers, Inc. Wheaton, IL 60189, USA. All rights reserved.

To purchase additional copies of this resource or other studies:
ORDER ONLINE at www.SerendipityHouse.com;
WRITE Serendipity House, 117 10th Avenue North, Nashville, TN 37234
FAX (615) 277-8181
PHONE (800) 525-9563

1-800-525-9563
www.SerendipityHouse.com

Printed in the United States of America

13 12 11 10 09 08 07   1 2 3 4 5 6 7 8 9 10

CONTENTS

SESSION	TITLE	PAGE

LEADER RESOURCES:

COMPANION CD FOR THE SECRET SEDUCTRESS!

PICK UP THE CD AT WWW.SERENDIPITYHOUSE.COM

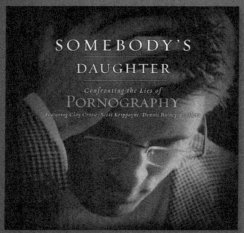

We designed this CD to be used as an integral part of the study The Secret Seductress. Be sure to pick up a copy for your group. Confront the lies of pornography with heart-transforming music, poetry, Scripture, interviews, and personal testimonies that grip the soul.

"Finally, someone has put sexual recovery to music! This CD has 19 tracks that are absolutely amazing. This well-produced music recovery CD is absolutely beneficial in the recovery process of sexual addiction. Every addict and partner of a sex addict will be amazed at how much insight and healing Somebody's Daughter has for his or her recovery."

– DR. DOUG WEISS, Heart2Heart Counseling Center, Colorado Springs, Colo.

PICKING UP THE PIECES RECOVERY STUDIES

Real help for real people living real life.

PICK UP THESE AND OTHER GREAT STUDIES AT WWW.SERENDIPITYHOUSE.COM ...

- Honest, experiential Bible studies that bind up the broken places and set captives free.

- Written by leading therapists and members of the American Association of Christian Counseling

- Great for support groups, recovery groups, church classes, accountability groups, and counseling centers

THE SECRET SEDUCTRESS:
BREAKING THE DESTRUCTIVE CYCLE OF PORN

Daily we're exposed to a sexually-saturated media. Everywhere we turn we're confronted and challenged by the sexual issues and brokenness that seeps into lives and families. Our sexual integrity is at risk. We must address the epidemic of sexual addiction if we're to be successful in restoring those who have fallen victim to its power and in preventing others from being caught in the snare. The church is waging a war on sexual addiction and sexual immorality ... and we're losing! Pornography is not a respecter of persons. It's as common in the Christian community as in the culture.

Pornography can be exhilarating in the moment like a drug high. For many men, porn is their drug of choice, and they find the arousal effective, at least temporarily, in getting the blood pumping, the pulse racing, and the adrenaline flowing, all of which can temporarily provide escape and comfort. But when the drug effect wears off immediately after climax, arousal is replaced by shame, and prowess is replaced by feelings of emptiness. The drug doesn't just wear off, it retaliates!

The reason so many men get sucked into pornography and then become trapped is that our typical approaches only act as triage, stopping the initial bleeding. Healing from sexual addictions is not as simple as just pulling a plug and everything is fixed. Sex addictions are a symptom of deeper emotional and spiritual issues. If the deeper issues are not addressed, sooner or later the plug will just be reconnected. We must delve into the wounds of the heart with God and then learn alternative, healthy ways to find the love and nurture we need.

PULLING THE PLUG PROCESS AND KEY QUESTIONS

DO I WANT TO GET WELL?

What am I thirsty for?

How can I break the cycle?

How will I counterattack?

What are my deepest longings?

Am I willing to embrace my pain?

What will be my legacy?

The Secret Seductress is an incredible resource for use men's groups, soul care groups, individual therapy sessions, and therapeutic groups.

WHAT'S AT STAKE?

BREAKING THE ICE - 15 MINUTES

LEADER: Be sure to read the introductory material in the front of this book and the leader's material at the end of the book. These "Breaking the Ice" exercises and questions are designed to help put people at ease and get them talking. Encourage group members to get acquainted with one another as you kick off this first group meeting. Keep the tone of the conversation light, and be sure that everyone has an opportunity to share.

THREE TRUTHS AND A LIE

LEADER INSTRUCTIONS FOR THE GROUP EXPERIENCE: Give each person a 3x5 card or a small sheet of paper and a pen. Read together the instructions preceding question 1. After allowing a couple of minutes to write, go around the group and ask each person to share his four statements. Then have the group try to guess which of the statements was the lie. Acknowledge the person who is the best at identifying lies. Congratulate his or her ability to discern the truth. After everyone has had a turn, ask the following questions:

On your cards, write four statements about yourself. The catch is that only three of the statements can be true. One should be completely made up. Come up with details of you life that are likely unknown to the others. The statements can be simple (I have lived in Florida; Pizza is my favorite food). But the more creative the statements are, the better (I once met Michael Jordan in an airport; I have whitewater rafted the Snake River). Just make sure the statements are believable ("I once chased a grizzly bear up a tree" is entertaining, but not very convincing).

1. Who told the most outrageous lie?

2. What was the most outrageous truth you heard?

3. Who was the most believable liar? Why was he so convincing?

4. What gave most people away? How much difference did it make how well you knew each person?

LEADER: *After the questions are answered, hold up your Bible. Say something like, "In my hands I hold a book that has been more used, more abused, more studied, and more scrutinized than any other literary work in history. Some call it a lie. Others think it tells half-truths. But this book changes lives more than any other. Today we're going to begin unmasking some of the key lies we've believed by shining the light of God's truth on them."*

5. Take turns introducing yourselves. Share your name, something about yourself, and one reason you joined this group.

Opening Prayer

God, we're not altogether sure how some areas of our lives got so far out of control, but we're thankful that You know us better than we know ourselves and that You know the path to freedom and healing. Thanks for each person in this group who will join us on the healing journey. Help us, even in this first session, to have a growing sense of Your presence and a growing sense of community with one another.

Objectives for this Session

- Discuss sexual dysfunction and the prevalence of pornography and sexual addiction in history and in our culture
- Discover what's at stake with the distortion of sexuality and sex addictions
- Expose current myths about sexuality and how the Enemy works to pervert God's original design
- Begin the journey toward self-awareness and sexual healing

DISCOVERING THE TRUTH – 35 MINUTES

LEADER: Explain that "Discovering the Truth" today provides understanding of key issues in pornography, sex addiction, and healing through looking at what God says and discussing our life experiences. Ask for volunteers to read Bible passages aloud. Be sure to leave time for the "Embracing the Truth" and "Connecting" segments that follow.

TRADING THE REAL THING FOR FAKES

Everyone struggles to some degree with sexuality. Sexual dysfunction has become a common cancer. Our 21st century culture bombards us with sexual messages. Families and children are devastated by sexual abuse and addictions. Leaders of our churches are falling prey. In New Testament times, people were just as challenged to keep themselves sexually pure. We find references throughout the Apostle Paul's writings to sexually addictive practices. Let's look at his words to the Roman and Corinthian churches ...

[24] So God said, in effect, "If that's what you want, that's what you get." It wasn't long before they were living in a pigpen, smeared with filth, filthy inside and out. [25] And all this because they traded the true God for a fake god, and worshiped the god they made instead of the God who made them—the God we bless, the God who blesses us. Oh, yes!

[26] Worse followed. Refusing to know God, they soon didn't know how to be human either—women didn't know how to be women, men didn't know how to be men. [27] Sexually confused, they abused and defiled one another, women with women, men with men—all lust, no love. And then they paid for it, oh, how they paid for it—emptied of God and love, godless and loveless wretches.

[28] Since they didn't bother to acknowledge God, God quit bothering them and let them run loose. [29] And then all hell broke loose ...

ROMANS 1:24-29A, THE MESSAGE

[9] Do you not know that the unjust will not inherit God's kingdom? Do not be deceived: no sexually immoral people, idolaters, adulterers, male prostitutes, homosexuals, [10] thieves, greedy people, drunkards, revilers, or swindlers will inherit God's kingdom.

1 CORINTHIANS 6:9-10, HCSB

LEADER: Discuss as many discovery questions as time permits. Encourage participation by inviting different individuals to respond. Read the questions and explanations for the group. It will help to highlight in advance the questions you don't want to miss.

1. According to Romans 1 and 1 Corinthians 6, what sexually unhealthy or addictive behaviors were going on in those societies and churches? Are you surprised by the list? Explain.

2. Compare the behaviors described in Rome and Corinth with behaviors and issues we hear reported today?

3. What appears to be the first major step of the Romans' slide into sexual addictions? (See Romans 1:24-26)? Why do you think this issue is so key?

4. What connections do you see from someone's spiritual and emotional conditions to his physical behaviors?

5. According to Romans 1:27-29, what was the outcome when God "let them run loose"?

The Cultural Assault

On a daily basis, we're exposed to a sexually-saturated media. Everywhere we turn we're confronted and challenged by the sexual perversion and brokenness that seeps into lives and families. Our sexual integrity is at risk. As a result, we must address the epidemic of sexual addiction if we're to be successful in restoring those who have fallen victim to its power and in preventing others from being caught in the snare.

6. About how many people do you know personally who struggle in this area? What kind of consequences do you see and imagine could be the result of inappropriate or unhealthy sexual behaviors?

Perhaps the major factor that's increasing the number of people struggling to maintain their sexual integrity is pornography. Our society is actually being sexually abused by the exposure to pornographic material. Pornography is the number one selling product on the Internet today. It is suggested that $10 billion is spent annually on pornography. [1]

7. What conclusions might we draw about the vast amount of money spent on pornography? How broad do you think this problem is in our culture? In our churches?

Cybersex and Internet pornography are classified as the new sexual addictions. It is estimated that at least 100,000 individuals visit the top five free porn sites on the Internet on a daily basis.

8. What are some reasons Internet porn is so prevalent and more attractive than picking up "adult" material at local convenience stores or frequenting X-rated establishments?

Several factors make the Internet a powerful and dangerous source of addiction. Psychologist Al Cooper describes the Triple-A Engine: It's Accessible, it's Affordable, and its users remain Anonymous [2] (or so we think until we're caught).

VITAL STATISTICS

The truth is that the church is waging a war on sexual addiction and sexual immorality ... and we're losing! Pornography is not a respecter of persons. The use of porn is just as common within the Christian community as it is in the society at large.

- Experts speculate that up to 10% of the Christian population in the U.S. is sexually addicted.

- Perhaps as many as 50% of all men in our churches today are struggling with pornography or other destructive sexual behaviors like masturbation and adultery.

- Even key spiritual leaders are trapped by pornography and sexual addiction. All too often the news reports inappropriate sexual behavior and unholy relationships among clergy and other religious leaders.

- According to Bsafe Online, 9 out of 10 children from ages 8 to 16 have been exposed to pornography on the Internet. [3]

THE SPIRITUAL ASSAULT

[26] Then God said, "Let Us make man in Our image, according to Our likeness ... [27] God created man in His own image, in the image of God He created him; male and female He created them.

GENESIS 1:26-27, NASB

[23] The man said, "This is now bone of my bones and flesh of my flesh; she shall be called 'woman,' for she was taken out of man." [24] For this reason a man will leave his father and mother and be united to his wife, and they will become one flesh.

GENESIS 2:23-24, NIV

9. God the Father, Son, and Holy Spirit are one in likeness and essence. According to Genesis 1:27, how does God's creation of mankind reflect His image?

10. What's significant, according to Genesis 2:24, about woman being created from man's essence? How does the relationship of husband and wife reflect the image of God?

[Jesus praying:] [22] The glory which You have given Me I have given to them, that they may be one, just as We are one; [23] I in them and You in Me, that they may be perfected in unity, so that the world may know that You sent Me, and loved them, even as You have loved Me.

JOHN 17:22-23A, NASB

We've discussed the force of the world's distorted values on our personal desires, which in turn affect our choices. But the third force is the real villain in the story. The Bible says that the evil one is God's enemy, who wants to destroy Him and us.

11. Understanding the creation of man and marriage in Genesis and Jesus' intent for unity in John 17, why do you suppose our enemy would put so much focus on distorting sexuality?

Whatever God creates, Satan tries to pervert or destroy. From the beginning of time, God created sex as a beautiful expression of physical intimacy between a husband and wife. God created male and female to reflect His image and glory. Sex is a wonderful physical, emotional, and spiritual expression of the oneness of God. Satan has deceived our society to the point that sexuality is not even close to what God originally intended.

EMBRACING THE TRUTH – 20 MINUTES

> **LEADER:** *This section focuses on helping group members integrate what they've learned from the Bible and discussions into their own hearts and lives. Be aware that the level of woundedness, fear, and addiction will be different for each person, so the rate of life application and healing will vary.*

SEXUAL MYTHOLOGY

We've discussed three powerful forces working to distort our sexuality and the oneness God created for us to share with Him and with our spouses. Those three forces are: our distorted desires, the world, and our enemy Satan. These forces have conspired to create a number of myths about sexuality. Let's look at 10 of these:

1. For each myth, discuss how prevalent it is and what the corresponding truth is.

   MYTH 1: SEX = LOVE.
   - Prevalence:
   - Real Truth:

   MYTH 2: SEX IS NO BIG DEAL; OUR GENITALS ARE DISCONNECTED FROM OUR SOULS.
   - Prevalence:
   - Real Truth:

Myth 3: Sex is always okay if it's mutual or consensual.
  - Prevalence:
  - Real Truth:

Myth 4: Sex should always be enjoyable and exciting.
  - Prevalence:
  - Real Truth:

Myth 5: There's nothing wrong with dominating, aggressive, angry sex.
  - Prevalence:
  - Real Truth:

Myth 6: The grass is greener outside of marriage.
  - Prevalence:
  - Real Truth:

Myth 7: Sex can meet our deepest needs and desires.
  - Prevalence:
  - Real Truth:

Myth 8: Homosexuality is just as normal as heterosexuality; it's all a matter of sexual preference.
  - Prevalence:
  - Real Truth:

Myth 9: We need to "kick the tires" to ensure compatibility in marriage.
  - Prevalence:
  - Real Truth:

Myth 10: Pornography doesn't hurt anybody.
  - Prevalence:
  - Real Truth:

2. What affects can pornography have in the emotional, spiritual, and relational life of an individual who views pornography? On others in his life?

Later in this study, we'll continue discussions of the powerful factors that influence our individual sexual development: (1) our family system, (2) traumatic events in our developmental years, and (3) the culture.

CONNECTING – 20 MINUTES

LEADER: Use "Connecting" as a time to help group members connect with one another, with God, and with their own hearts. Be prepared to share your story first to set the tone of openness and trust. Those who are slower to open up will benefit greatly from hearing your story and the stories of others. Invite everyone to join into the discussions.

VOICES OF DECEPTION

The culture bombards us with myths and deceptions about sex and also about ourselves. Jesus spoke strongly about the deceiver who plants so many lies in our world and in our hearts when He said:

You belong to your father, the devil, and you want to carry out your father's desire. He was a murderer from the beginning, not holding to the truth, for there is no truth in him. When he lies, he speaks his native language, for he is a liar and the father of lies.

JOHN 8:44, NIV

1. What does Jesus identify as the native language of the devil? What does He indicate happens to us when we believe the lies of the Enemy?

In the epic story *Lord of the Rings*, a small, peaceful, forest hobbit named Frodo is chosen to carry a powerful, evil ring to the land of Mordor—the only place the ring can be destroyed—to stop the dark lord from enslaving all of middle earth. He's accompanied on this dangerous journey by his closest friend Sam and a creature named Gollum. Gollum was once an innocent creature named Sméagol, but over decades the evil power of the ring had warped his physical appearance and his heart so that he'd become ugly and evil. The ring had a powerful hold on anyone who carried it, and it was the constant object of Gollum's desire, which he called "my precious." In the following scene the dual personalities represent the battle going on inside Gollum.

LEADER INSTRUCTIONS FOR THE GROUP EXPERIENCE: Have a TV/DVD player set up. Read the preceding introduction to the group, and then show the clip from the second Lord of the Rings film, The Two Towers. *On DVD-2, show Chapter 29 from the Special Extended Edition (1:38:35 to 1:41:05 minutes on the DVD timer) entitled "Gollum and Sméagol." On the Standard DVD Version, it's Chapter 22. After showing the clip, discuss these questions:*

2. What are the various tactics Gollum uses to deceive Sméagol? Why are they so effective? What feelings is Gollum exploiting to gain advantage?

3. Which of these deceptions has the Enemy whispered in your ear about you or your sex addictions? Check all that apply, and then briefly share your experience with the group.

   ❒ Need—Sex, my addiction, is critical to my survival: "must have the precious."
   ❒ Fear—I won't be able to cope without it.
   ❒ Inferiority—I'm a bad, unworthy person: "nobody likes you anyway."
   ❒ Isolation—I'm all alone anyway so it's up to me to take care of me: "You don't have any friends." "Where would you be without me?"
   ❒ Failures—You're a failure anyway so why even try?
   ❒ Shame—You're behaviors and addictions are the truest thing about you.
   ❒ Self-hatred—You should loathe yourself for who you are and what you do.
   ❒ Escape—You must find a way to avoid the pain and isolation.
   ❒ Other: _____ .

4. How has the culture affected your personal sexuality and beliefs about sex? What are tools that the world and the Enemy use to grab people's attention?

5. Which of the following do you find most influential in your own life when it comes to sexual stimulation:

   ❒ Television shows   ❒ Movies
   ❒ Print media   ❒ The Internet
   ❒ Billboards   ❒ Music
   ❒ Overtly sexual clothing   ❒ Emotional connection with someone at work
   ❒ Other: _____

Gollum gives voice to Sméagol's addictions—his past distorted beliefs and familiar patterns of behavior. Gollum says, "I saved us. It was me. We survived because of me!" Sméagol did survive because of Gollum. His sneaking, lying, stealing, and treachery allowed him to survive but robbed him of his life.

Let's pray that each of us would see the truth about our lives and our problems in this coming week. Let's pray, too, for the lies or myths with which each of us is struggling. How can we pray for you today?

MY PRAYER NEEDS:

MY GROUP'S PRAYER NEEDS:

LEADER: Thank people for coming and for their desire to find freedom in their lives. Let them know that you and the leadership team are available 24/7 for support. Be sure to give an overview of the "Taking It Home" assignment for the coming week.

TAKING IT HOME

LEADER: Explain that the "Taking It Home" section each week will contain an introspective question to ask of your heart or a question to take to God. There may also be other questions or activities to help you on your healing journey. Strongly encourage everyone to spend time absorbing the truths learned today and completing the assignments for the week, including review of the Group Covenant on page 18 (you'll discuss this next week).

QUESTIONS TO TAKE TO MY HEART

The following questions ask you to look into your heart and focus on your deepest feelings about yourself. Our behaviors are the best indicators of what we really believe deep down. Look deep into the underlying beliefs in your heart where your truest attitudes and motives live. (See Psalm 51:6.) Spend time reflecting, and don't settle for a quick answer. Be sure to capture your thoughts.

> ✳ Look back over the questions in the "Embracing the Truth" and "Connecting" sections. What lies have I embraced that might be driving my addictive behaviors and my unwillingness open up or ask for the help I need?

> ✳ How has using pornography affected my relationship with God? How about my relationships with people close to me? How might my spouse feel if she discovers that I've been viewing pornography?

JOURNAL EXERCISE

During Session 1 we've discussed how we're bombarded with sexual messages and stimuli. Use the journal space on page 19 to jot down a record of all the sexual triggers or stimuli you encounter for at least one of the days before the next group meeting. Then, next to each stimulus, jot down your physical and emotional responses to that stimulus or trigger.

ENDNOTES:

1 "Vital Statistics," BSafe Online [cited 29 November 2006]. Available on the Internet: http://www.bsafehome. com/vitalfacts.asp.

2 Al Cooper, David Delmonico, and Ron Berg, "Cybersex Users, Abusers, and Compulsives: New Findings and Implications," Sexual Addiction and Compulsivity 7, nos. 1 and 2, 2000.

3 "Vital Statistics," BSafe Online [cited 29 November 2006]. Available on the Internet: http://www.bsafehome. com/vitalfacts.asp.

GROUP COVENANT

As you begin this study, it is important that your group covenant together, agreeing to live out important group values. Once these values are agreed upon, your group will be on its way to experiencing true redemptive community. It's very important that your group discuss these values—preferably as you begin this study.

* PRIORITY: While we are in this group, we will give the group meetings priority. All the sessions are integrated, with each session building on the sessions that precede them. Committed attendance is vital to overcoming your addictions.

  NOTE: Due to the focus of this group on taking the journey to freedom, group sessions will require a full 90 minutes to complete, so plan accordingly.

* PARTICIPATION AND FAIRNESS: Because we are here to receive help, we commit to participation and interaction in the group. No one dominates. We will be fair to others and concentrate on telling our own stories briefly.

* HOMEWORK: The homework experiences are an integral and vital part of the recovery process. The assignments between each session might include: (1) A Question to Take to My Heart; (2) A Question to Take to God; and (3) Activities that must be completed to continue on with your healing journey.

* RESPECT AND OWNERSHIP: Everyone is given the right to his or her own opinions, and all questions are encouraged and respected. We will not judge or condemn as others share their stories. We are each responsible for our own recovery and will not "own" someone else's. Offensive language is not permitted.

* CONFIDENTIALITY: Anything said in our meetings is never repeated outside the meeting without permission of all of group members. This is vital in creating the environment of trust and openness required to facilitate the healing and freedom. Names of attendees will not be shared with others. NOTE: Check state and federal laws governing pastoral and counselor reporting requirements for any known criminal activities.

* LIFE CHANGE: We will regularly assess our progress and will complete the "Taking it Home" activities to reinforce what we are learning and better integrate those lessons into our personal journeys.

* CARE AND SUPPORT: Permission is given to call upon each other at any time, especially in times of crisis. The group will provide care for every member.

* ACCOUNTABILITY AND INTEGRITY: We agree to let the members of our group hold us accountable to commitments we make in whatever loving ways we decide upon. Unsolicited advice giving is not permitted. We will seek out and build a close relationship with accountability partners for mutual growth and responsibility.

* EXPECTATIONS OF FACILITATORS: This meeting is not professional therapy. We are not licensed therapists. Group facilitators are volunteers whose only desire is to encourage people in finding freedom and hope.

I agree to all of the above_____ Date:_____

Sexual Triggers, Stimuli, and Response Journal

DO I WANT TO GET WELL?

BREAKING THE ICE – 15 MINUTES

LEADER: Encourage each group member to respond to the "Breaking the Ice" questions. These questions are designed to help group members get to know each other better, while getting them used to hearing their own voices. The more connected group members are, the more open and healing the group will become. Keep the tone of these questions light and fun. Choose only two of the first three questions to save time.

1. Which of the following identifies your least favorite health-conscious activity? Why did you choose that answer?

   ❐ Eating vegetarian pizza
   ❐ Running, jogging, or bouncing—depending on my body's current condition
   ❐ Enduring "pain and torture" at a gym or health club
   ❐ What do you mean "no steak and potatoes"?!
   ❐ One word: tofu
   ❐ Dancing the pounds away to a Richard Simmons or aerobics conditioning video
   ❐ Mourning the loss of banana splits and chocolate
   ❐ Other: _____

2. Which food would your close friends and family say best describes your typical approach to decision-making and self-discipline? Why?

   ❐ Waffle—you're up, you're down, no you're up ...
   ❐ Cracker—when any pressure is applied, you crumble
   ❐ Oatmeal—the longer it sets, the harder it becomes
   ❐ Steak—subject it to the fire and it just keeps getting tougher
   ❐ Roadkill—no matter what you decide to do with it, it always stinks
   ❐ Tossed Salad—you're usually mixed up, but you're colorful
   ❐ Caviar—it might make you feel good, but it's going to cost you
   ❐ Other: _____

3. What was something you thought you wanted or needed until you actually got it? Briefly share your story with the group.

4. What did you notice as you paid close attention this week to the sexual stimuli and messages you encountered in your daily life?

5. How did your "Taking It Home" questions go? As you listened to your heart this week, what did you discover about the lies you've believed or about the effects of pornography on your relationships?

OPENING PRAYER

God, our loving Father, join us today. We want to see things through Your eyes. We admit that we have not done such a great job of running our own lives. Because of forces we can't see and are not equipped to fight, we keep getting dragged back into destructive, addictive cycles over and over. We're tired of quick short-term fixes; we need Your supernatural power in our lives. Please make Your presence real to us today.

OBJECTIVES FOR THIS SESSION

- Contrast God's perspectives on healthy sexuality with sexual addiction
- Identify the process and key questions to answer to move toward freedom
- Understand that remaining sexually pure is a matter of willingness versus willfulness
- Recognize and release our double-mindedness about getting well
- Grapple with the implications of the Bible's warnings about "one flesh union" and "sins against our own body"
- Realize that the Enemy attacks where we are most in need and most vulnerable

DISCOVERING THE TRUTH – 30 MINUTES

LEADER: *In "Discovering the Truth," ask various group members to read the Bible passages aloud. Encourage everyone to participate and allow people to discover new truths through the discussions, but keep things moving. You'll also want to allow time for "Embracing the Truth" questions and the "Connecting" group experience that follow.*

HEALTHY SEX AND DESTRUCTIVE SEX

Our culture and the Christian church are experiencing a great deal of turmoil in the area of sexuality. There are essentially two primary areas of struggle:

(1) Inhibited sexual desire – God's desire for a person's sexual life remains elusive and hurtful.

(2) Sexual compulsion – Forceful, difficult to control urges drive people into secret lives of shame and self-hatred because they can't even live out their own values. This is the realm of the sex addict.

1. What's the difference in your mind between healthy sexuality and sexual addiction? What do you think should be the goal of healing for someone struggling with a destructive or unhealthy sexual problem?

2. In your personal view, what's the purpose of sex?

The goal of freedom from sexual addiction is not like that of other addictions such as alcoholism, which has a goal of abstinence. The goal for sex addicts is healthy sexual processing and expression along with healthy corresponding relationships. The difference between healthy sexuality and sexual addiction is not about experiencing sexual feelings, but rather how we express them. The following chart provides an overview of the differences.

BEHAVIOR & THOUGHTS	SEX ADDICT	NON-SEX ADDICT
Thinks about sex	Constantly	Periodically
Encounters sexual stimuli, such as pornography or an attractive person	Initiates a cycle of sexual thoughts and hoped-for sex activities. Disregards all moral/spiritual boundaries	Acknowledges the stimulus and may even be aroused, but considers and regards all moral and spiritual boundaries.
Masturbation	Becomes a habitual pattern used to medicate feelings	Does not allow it to become a pattern or source of comfort
Experience of sexual sin	Goes through a cycle of guilt and shame but repeats the sin.	Confesses, turns away from, and learns from the experience.
Marital sexuality	Selfish use of spouse to meet needs, including the need to avoid feelings and intimacy.	Finds fulfillment in meeting needs of spouse as much or more than self. Experiences deep levels of emotional and spiritual intimacy.

3. What key insight or new perspective from this chart stands out to you?

PULLING THE PLUG SCHEMATIC

Healing from sexual addictions is not as simple as just pulling a plug and everything is fixed. Sex addictions are one expression of deeper emotional and spiritual issues. If the deeper issues are not addressed, sooner or later the plug will just be reconnected. Your healing journey will continue well beyond this study of *The Secret Seductress*, but wrestling with each of these seven key questions is vital to freedom and healing. Our focus in Session 2 is addressing the question: "Do I want to get well?"

DO I WANT TO GET WELL?

What am I thirsty for?
How can I break the cycle?
How will I counterattack?
What are my deepest longings?
Am I willing to embrace my pain?
What will be my legacy?

Do You Want to Get Well?

One of the most important questions a person will want to consider on the road of recovery from addiction to pornography is "Do you want to get well?"

² By the Sheep Gate in Jerusalem there is a pool, called Bethesda in Hebrew, which has five colonnades. ³ Within these lay a multitude of the sick—blind, lame, and paralyzed—waiting for the moving of the water, ⁴ because an angel would go down into the pool from time to time and stir up the water. Then the first one who got in after the water was stirred up recovered from whatever ailment he had. ⁵ One man was there who had been sick for 38 years.

⁶ When Jesus saw him lying there and knew he had already been there a long time, He said to him, "Do you want to get well?"

⁷ "Sir," the sick man answered, "I don't have a man to put me into the pool when the water is stirred up, but while I'm coming, someone goes down ahead of me."

⁸ "Get up," Jesus told him, "pick up your bedroll and walk!"
⁹ Instantly the man got well, picked up his bedroll, and started to walk.

JOHN 5:2-9A, HCSB

4. Why had the paralyzed man waited at the pool of Bethesda for 38 years? What do think his attitude must have been after wasting away there all that time?

5. Of all the compassionate questions Jesus could have asked, why do you suppose he asked, "Do you want to get well?" (The man's answer in verse 7 gives some clues.)

It seems the man had adopted the identity of his condition (being paralyzed). Jesus knew that for the man to be healed, he had to want to change. Staying pure is as much a matter of *willingness* to change as it is *willfulness* to follow through. James gives more insight into this willingness and willfulness factors:

⁵ If any of you lacks wisdom, he should ask God, who gives generously to all without finding fault, and it will be given to him. ⁶ But when he asks, he must believe and not doubt, because he who doubts is like a wave of the sea, blown and tossed by the wind. ⁷ That man should not think he will receive anything from the Lord; ⁸ he is a double-minded man, unstable in all he does.

JAMES 1:5-8, NIV

6. According to James 1:5, what can we do when we find ourselves in a situation that we don't fully understand or with which we don't know how to cope? How is God likely to respond to us?

7. In what ways might a man be "double-minded" about pornography and other sex addictions (see verses 6-8)?

There's always a part of us that wants to get well—to find freedom from addiction. However, there's also a part of us that enjoys the pleasure of sexually acting out. That's why so many people must hit rock bottom before they are really ready for change. Until we're ready to forsake our secret seductresses and decide that we want with all of our hearts to get well, we'll be unwilling to make the changes required to heal. To recover from porn addiction and achieve sexual purity means you must be committed to do whatever it takes to stay pure and clean despite massive influences to the contrary.

EMBRACING THE TRUTH – 25 MINUTES

> LEADER: *This section focuses on helping group members integrate what they've learned from the Bible and group discussions into their own hearts and lives. The focus is on the dangerous choices we make and the our powerlessness to stop our addictive behaviors on our own.*

PLAYING WITH FIRE

The truth is that every person in this group is participating because we know at some level that we're playing with fire or we're worried about our temptations to play with fire.

15 Do you not know that your bodies are the members of Christ? So should I take the members of Christ and make them members of a prostitute? Absolutely not! 16 Do you not know that anyone joined to a prostitute is one body with her? For it says, "The two will become one flesh." 17 But anyone joined to the Lord is one spirit with Him. 18 Flee from sexual immorality! "Every sin a person can commit is outside the body," but the person who is sexually immoral sins against his own body.

1 CORINTHIANS 6:15-18, HCSB

1. According to verses 16 and 18, why do sexual activities outside of marriage get so complicated?

2. According to verse 18, what is it about sexual sins that make them distinct from other sins—both in our relationships and at a deeper level within our souls?

[Referring to sexual activities outside of marriage] 27 Can a man scoop fire into his lap without his clothes being burned? 28 Can a man walk on hot coals without his feet being scorched?

PROVERBS 6:27-28, NIV

3. What negative consequences might somebody eventually face who "scoops fire into his lap"?

In his letter to the Corinthians, Paul stressed that sexual relations involve deep soul-level union. Sex is more than skin deep; the man and woman actually become "one flesh"—unified physically, emotionally, and spiritually. In *The Screwtape Letters*, C.S. Lewis writes, "Every time a man and a woman enter into a sexual relationship a spiritual bond is established between them which must be eternally enjoyed or eternally endured." [1]

The sexual drive hungers for personal satisfaction and progresses like no other drive. Sex outside the boundaries it was created for—oneness in marriage—also has a way of destroying a person like no other sin. The inappropriate use of sexual intimacy progresses in destroying us at the deepest human level. As we continue to "scoop fire into our laps," eventually we'll get burned, and badly. That's why God warns us to run away from it!

POWERLESS

Sooner or later, the sexual activities we turn to for pleasure or escape will control us, and we'll become enslaved and powerless to someone or something. Listen to the Apostle Paul as he describes the battle going on inside each of us ...

[18] *I know that nothing good lives in me, that is, in my flesh. For the desire to do what is good is with me, but there is no ability to do it.* [19] *For I do not do the good that I want to do, but I practice the evil that I do not want to do.* [20] *Now if I do what I do not want, I am no longer the one doing it, but it is the sin that lives in me.*

ROMANS 7:18-20, HCSB

4. How would you describe the inner struggle Paul highlights in Romans 7:18-20? Even though we fear many consequences, why do we find it so difficult to give up destructive sexual behaviors?

Paul is very aware of what's going on inside himself and inside each of us. He further explains:

[21] *... when I want to do good, evil is with me.* [22] *For in my inner self I joyfully agree with God's law.* [23] *But I see a different law in the parts of my body, waging war against the law of my mind and taking me prisoner to the law of sin in the parts of my body.* [24] *What a wretched man I am! Who will rescue me from this body of death?*

ROMANS 7:21-24, HCSB

5. Even a great man like the Apostle Paul struggled—he was human. What emotions do you think he was feeling as he wrote verses 21-24? What did Paul realize about himself and the power he had over the assaults on his mind and heart?

6. After Paul admits sin is unmanageable and that we're powerless over it, what does he cry out for (verse 24)? Tell about a time when you faced sexual temptation, pulled in two directions. How do you feel about the prospect of being powerless and relying on someone to rescue you?

Because of our humanness and the sin that lives in us, we're powerless to change ourselves. When they try, they may succeed for varying lengths of time by doing what therapists call "white knuckling" or "acting in." But denying the body does not bring healing; we only end up ignoring the real issues in an attempt to appease the God we believe is strict and vengeful. This inability to give up the illusion of control is precisely what prevents sex addicts from healing. Our attempts to control our lives prevent us from trusting God to care for us.

Unmanageability, escape from pain, shame, and—for many—some level of addiction are interwoven into the very fabric of sin. Sin is anything that pulls us out of relationship with God and results in behaviors that are destructive to ourselves or to others.

CONNECTING – 20 MINUTES

LEADER: Use "Connecting" as a time to help group members connect with one another, with God, and with their own hearts. Be prepared to share your story first to set the tone of openness and trust. Those who are slower to open up will benefit greatly from hearing your story and the stories of others. Invite everyone to join into the discussions.

PRESSURE INSIDE AND OUT

1. What pressures or influences do you experience "out in the world" that pull you into pornography or other inappropriate, destructive sexual behaviors?

On top of all the outside pressure, we also struggle with pressures from within ourselves that seem at times impossible to control.

2. Have you used pornography for self comfort to escape difficult emotions such as loneliness, anxiety, fear, hurt, or anger? Share an example with the group.

WHAT HARM COULD IT DO?

It's all too easy to find an excuse to justify looking at pornography. Perhaps a spouse said no to sexual advances one night so you justified sexual gratification using pronography. Reasoning "my wife isn't available, and surfing the Web for pornography isn't really hurting anybody," you spend the next two hours burning images into your mind.

Earlier, we discussed that sex is more than skin deep—the man and woman actually become "one flesh" physically, emotionally, and spiritually (1 Corinthians 6:16-17). The song "Is it Me?" helps us see how a wife, fiancé, or even girlfriend can be deeply hurt by our use of pornography.

LEADER INSTRUCTIONS FOR THE GROUP EXPERIENCE: Page 4 shows a companion music CD called Somebody's Daughter *available from Serendipity House. Have a CD player queued up to play the song "Is It Me?" from that CD. If you like, you can download lyrics from* www.SerendipityHouse.com/Community *(under Group Leaders - Leadership Aids). Ask group members to close their eyes and listen. Give a few moments for personal reflection at the end of the song and then discuss the following questions:*

---

3. What tough questions and deep wounds did you hear the woman wrestling with in this song?

4. How do think your beloved would be affected if she somehow found out about your secret seductress? How would it affect your family? Your other relationships?

5. What would it be like for you to discover your wife was posing nude on the Internet or fixated on the size of another man's genitals? How would that affect your relationship?

The question's often asked, "Why should I give up pornography since I'm not actually involved with another person?" Many have the attitude that because porn doesn't "cross the flesh line" it's okay. Because it does "cross the one-flesh line," your wife will feel betrayed when she discovers you're involved with pornography, just as you would if she was engrossed with the naked body of another man. Most women also begin the comparison game asking, "Is it me? Am I not enough? What's wrong with me?" The relationship is tremendously damaged. Often the hurt is as deep as the hurt of uncovering an affair.

Without a doubt, God can and does heal men from addiction to pornography and other destructive sexual behaviors. To find freedom and healing though, we have to find healing from our hurts and anger from the past, grab hold of God, and develop new coping strategies to deal with the challenges in life. Underlying all this, we need to learn alternative, healthy ways to find the love and nurture we need. Finding freedom is a process, but it all begins with a heart that is single-mindedly determined to get well.

> *LEADER: Be aware that this may have been a difficult session for some in your group. Be sure to emphasize the hope that each man will experience freedom and healing as you take this journey together. Encourage openness by sharing your own struggles first. Focus on prayer requests specific to breaking the destructive cycle of porn.*

My Prayer Needs:

My Group's Prayer Needs:

RISKS JOURNAL

WHAT AM I THIRSTY FOR?

BREAKING THE ICE – 20 MINUTES

> LEADER: "Breaking the Ice" is designed to help group members settle into the group setting and to put them at ease when talking about the session topic. You may choose to skip the first question to save some time.

1. Which water activity would be most appealing to you? Least appealing?

- ❏ White-water rafting on the Upper Galley River
- ❏ Boat ride at the base of Niagara Falls
- ❏ Surfing in Hawaii
- ❏ Floating the day away at a water park
- ❏ Cliff diving in Acapulco
- ❏ Hunting alligators on Lake Okeechobee
- ❏ Canoeing down the Amazon River
- ❏ Relaxing in a hot tub after skiing in the Alps
- ❏ Scuba diving in Cancun
- ❏ Swimming with dolphins in the Florida Keys
- ❏ Racing a speed boat on Lake Michigan
- ❏ Trout fishing in a Colorado mountain stream
- ❏ Other: _____

CRUNCH & CHUG COMPETITION

> LEADER INSTRUCTIONS FOR THE GROUP EXPERIENCE: Set up a competition between four two-person teams. One member of each team will be the Feeder and the other will be the Cruncher/Chugger. Each Cruncher/Chugger will be blindfolded and sitting with hands behind his backs. At the start signal, each Feeder will stuff six crackers into the mouth of his blindfolded partner. Once the crackers are consumed, the Feeder will hold the cup as his partner chugs the drink. The first team to consume both crackers and drink is declared the winner. You'll need the following supplies for the competition:

- Four blindfolds
- 24 salted crackers (6 per team)
- Team 1: Cup of fresh, cold water
- Team 2: Sport drink such as Gatorade®
- Team 3: Cold, carbonated cola
- Team 4: Cup of salt water
- A prize for the winning team
- Paper towels for cleaning up

Award a prize, then discuss the following questions:

2. What was the winning team's strategy? What helped this team to win?

At least two of the teams had thirst-quenching drinks. One team had a belch-producing drink. The final team chugged contaminated salt water.

3. Clearly, not all drinks quench our deep thirsts. What makes a drink a good thirst-quencher? What makes it a bad thirst-quencher? Why is it sometimes difficult to distinguish one from the other?

4. How did your "Taking It Home" assignment go this week? As you wrestled with whether you really want to get well, what did you find holding you back from being single-minded and willing to forsake your secret seductress?

5. Did you hear from God about His feelings toward pornography or your sexual acting out? Did He reveal how He feels about you personally? Share what you heard.

OPENING PRAYER

God, we're aware of some thirst inside us, some craving down deep that Gatorade® won't satisfy. We're here because we've misunderstood this craving. We're here because over and over we've lowered our buckets down into wells of contaminated water and then drunk like madmen. We've gotten sick from the water but confess that we haven't gotten sick of the water. Yesterday we failed in seclusion and secrecy. Today we seek healing in supportive brotherhood. Lead us, Lord, to the oasis of pure and living water that satisfies and heals.

OBJECTIVES FOR THIS SESSION

- Understand some reasons we turn to pornography and why it provides temporary relief
- Begin to recognize our deepest thirsts and longings
- Recognize conditions and emotions that make us most susceptible to misusing sex
- Begin to release the stranglehold of the past, lies of the Enemy, secrets, and denial
- Define sexual addictions
- Respond rightly to our masculine desire to be wildly intimate and wildly free

DISCOVERING THE TRUTH – 25 MINUTES

LEADER: *"Discovering the Truth" revolves around the story of a woman Jesus meets at Jacob's well in Samaria. Read the explanations aloud or ask for volunteers. Be sure to leave ample time for "Embracing the Truth" questions and the "Connecting" group experience that follow. Review the Pulling the Plug Schematic before diving in.*

In our last session, we focused on our willingness to get well. Our focus in Session 3 is asking ourselves what we're thirsty for.

DO I WANT TO GET WELL?
WHAT AM I THIRSTY FOR?

How can I break the cycle?
How will I counterattack?
What are my deepest longings?
Am I willing to embrace my pain?
What will be my legacy?

The Wrong Kind of Water

When we're thirsty, we get a drink. When we're tired, we get some rest. We all have needs and desires, but too often we don't really understand our needs, we try to satisfy desires that have become distorted, or we try to satisfy what we thirst for with the wrong drink.

1. Can you recall an achievement, an experience, or a purchase that you thought would be satisfying but in actuality it fell far short, either (1) producing only a brief buzz or high, or (2) exacting a very high cost emotionally, relationally, physically, spiritually, or financially? Explain.

You've probably heard tales of people being stranded at sea, who with no other source of water succumb to drinking the salt water, which only intensifies thirst and accelerates dehydration. For a brief moment, the cool seawater soothes the parched throat, but then the salt retaliates against the body. Even after vomiting, the man will rinse his mouth with more salt water and feel compelled to drink it again. He's thirsty. He desperately needs water and is cruelly surrounded by it—just the wrong kind.

2. How is pornography like salty seawater?

Deeper Thirsts

In John 4, Jesus encounters a woman at a well on the outskirts of Sychar in Samaria. This woman has a sordid past so she comes to draw water at noon to avoid the respectable women who gather early in the morning.

The conversation begins with the topic of actual water and physical thirst, but Jesus but quickly transitions to a discussion of deeper spiritual thirst and living water.

> LEADER: *Invite various group members to read parts of the story about Jesus and the Samaritan woman from John 4.*

7 Soon a Samaritan woman came to draw water, and Jesus said to her, "Please give me a drink." 8 He was alone at the time because his disciples had gone into the village to buy some food.

9 The woman was surprised, for Jews refuse to have anything to do with Samaritans. She said to Jesus, "You are a Jew, and I am a Samaritan woman. Why are you asking me for a drink?" …

16 "Go and get your husband," Jesus told her.

17 "I don't have a husband," the woman replied.

Jesus said, "You're right! You don't have a husband—18 for you have had five husbands, and you aren't even married to the man you're living with now. You certainly spoke the truth!"

19 "Sir," the woman said, "you must be a prophet."

JOHN 4:7-9,16-19, NLT

LEADER: *Discuss as many discovery questions as time permits. Encourage group members to try to imagine themselves in the position of the Samaritan woman. Read the questions and explanations for the group. It will help to highlight in advance the questions you don't want to miss.*

---

3. What did Jesus gently expose as the "water" the Samaritan woman was pursuing to quench her deepest thirsts (verse 17)? As she turned again and again to the "polluted water" that failed to satisfy her, how do you think she might have felt about herself, her life, and God?

4. The woman's needs and struggles cannot simply be reduced to sexual activity or promiscuity. After five failed marriages she is living with a man who is not her husband. What can we surmise about what the woman is really searching for?

Jesus did not see a five-time divorcee and town whore. He saw a woman with a parched soul—desperately thirsty to be loved by a man. After five failed marriages this woman had given up on finding a husband that would satisfy her deepest longing—she settled for a man who'll at least stay … for a while … in exchange for sex. In the midst of her loneliness, fear, desperation, shame, and failure Jesus offered hope and healing.

¹⁰ Jesus replied, "If you only knew the gift God has for you and who you are speaking to, you would ask me, and I would give you living water."

¹¹ "But sir, you don't have a rope or a bucket," she said, "and this well is very deep. Where would you get this living water? ¹² And besides, do you think you're greater than our ancestor Jacob, who gave us this well? How can you offer better water than he and his sons and his animals enjoyed?"

¹³ Jesus replied, "Anyone who drinks this water will soon become thirsty again. ¹⁴ But those who drink the water I give will never be thirsty again. It becomes a fresh, bubbling spring within them, giving them eternal life."

¹⁵ "Please, sir," the woman said, "give me this water! Then I'll never be thirsty again, and I won't have to come here to get water." ...

²³ But the time is coming—indeed it's here now—when true worshipers will worship the Father in spirit and in truth. The Father is looking for those who will worship him that way. ²⁴ For God is Spirit, so those who worship him must worship in spirit and in truth."

JOHN 4:10-15,23-24, NLT

5. Jesus told the woman she'd been turning to the wrong things to find meaning, value, acceptance, and intimacy. What is the "living water" that Jesus is offering in place of our counterfeit lovers and secret seductresses (verses 10 and 14)?

Jesus offers each of us a new life, filled with truth, healing, and freedom from our destructive behaviors and secret seductresses ... but we have to choose His water, accept His ways, and fight for our freedom in this life!

6. What does He tell us in verse 23 that we need to do in order to realize this new life?

Usually we respond according to the distorted desires we've become conditioned to fulfilling. Our "drug of choice" produces a sense of relief, comfort, release, or pleasure. This pattern is an addiction and it's a trap! To find freedom and life we must turn to Jesus. He alone can heal our pain and fill our hearts with the one thing we were born searching for—a deep and intimate relationship with Him. Believe Him, trust that His heart is good, and follow Him with all your heart, soul, mind, and strength.

The Samaritan woman finally discovered and embraced the thing for which she was truly thirsty. She set aside the lies she'd been living. She set aside her shame and self-loathing. She set aside her counterfeit lovers. She left her old water jar behind ...

²⁸ The woman left her water jar beside the well and ran back to the village, telling everyone, ²⁹ "Come and see a man who told me everything I ever did! Could he possibly be the Messiah?"

JOHN 4:28-29, NLT

EMBRACING THE TRUTH – 25 MINUTES

SECRETS, SHAME, AND SHADOWS

> LEADER: *This section focuses on helping group members integrate what they've learned from the Bible discussions into their own hearts and lives. As with the Samaritan woman, we must wrestle with some internal tensions if we're going to forsake our secret seductresses and turn to Jesus for intimacy and a life of fullness.*

It's clear that Jesus doesn't condone the Samaritan woman's past or current behavior. Yet Jesus doesn't condemn her because of her sin or failures. There is a creative tension between embracing God's forgiveness and stretching it to absurd lengths to minimize our sin. In John 8:11, Jesus reached out to another person caught in sexual sin, saying, "Neither do I condemn you. ... Go now and leave your life of sin" (NIV).

Jesus knows pursuing counterfeit lovers will destroy us, so He calls us to leave them. It's said, "God loves you just like you are. And He loves you too much to leave you that way."

1. What are some difficult emotions from which we try to escape through our secret seductresses or other addictive behaviors?

2. What are some reasons we struggle with the tension of being forgiven and accepted by Jesus? How about the tension of taking the healing journey with Jesus, yet risking the steps back into our shadows and secrets before we go forward?

[17] *For God did not send his Son into the world to condemn the world, but to save the world through him. ...* [20] *Everyone who does evil hates the light, and will not come into the light for fear that his deeds will be exposed.*

JOHN 3:17,20, NIV

[Jesus explained,] "You will know the truth, and the truth will set you free."   JOHN 8:32, HCSB

3. Discuss ways that secrets, shame, and shadows can block us from reaching the ongoing life, salvation (John 3:17-20), and freedom (John 8:32) that Jesus wants for each of us.

If truth is what sets you free, then what keeps you in bondage is deeply-embedded deception. If knowing and operating from truth is what brings freedom, then what enslaves us is living out of deeply-held, subtle lies that in turn drive our choices and behaviors. Most of the time the lies we've accepted are subterranean and unrecognized.

4. Discuss this statement from Henry Blackaby: "What you do in response to God's revelation (invitation) reveals what you believe about God." [1]

5. How can we identify deeply-held lies (our true beliefs) that have become so familiar we wear them as we would a comfortable pair of shoes?

> LEADER: *Share an example of a deeply-held lie such as, "I am totally useless and beyond God's redemption," or "If people really knew me they'd push me away or abandon me."*

INSIDE OUT CHANGE

Whether refinishing furniture, refurbishing a house, restoring an old car, or cleaning up a life, renewal requires the same three-step process:

Step 1 – Strip the veneer..
Step 2 – Identify and treat the wood.
Step 3 – Resurface and apply a new finish.

6. How would a piece of furniture or classic car look if you did only the first renewal step? Only the third step? How might this apply to renewing your mind with the truth?

[1] I urge you, brothers, in view of God's mercy, to offer your bodies as living sacrifices, holy and pleasing to God — this is your spiritual act of worship. [2] Do not conform any longer to the pattern of this world, but be transformed by the renewing of your mind. Then you will be able to test and approve what God's will is — his good, pleasing and perfect will.

ROMANS 12:1-2, NIV

[2] Wash me thoroughly from my iniquity and cleanse me from my sin. ... [6] Behold, You desire truth in the innermost being, and in the hidden part You will make me know wisdom.

PSALM 51:2,6, NASB

7. Why does God focus so much on "renewing our minds" and "truth in our innermost being"? What do you expect would happen if you only worked to change your behavior without making internal changes to your heart and mind?

CONNECTING – 20 MINUTES

LEADER: Use "Connecting" as a time to help group members connect with each other, with God, and with their own hearts. The song "Into the Light" will set the tone for breaking the bonds of secrets, shame, and shadows. As always, be prepared to share your story first to set the tone of openness and trust. Those who are slower to open up will benefit greatly from hearing your story and the stories of others. Encourage the group to accept everyone as God does ... right where we are now.

INTO THE LIGHT

Jesus said, "Everyone who does evil hates the light" (John 3:20) More than anything the Enemy wants to hold us captive by keeping us in secrets, shame, and shadows. Freedom comes with love, acceptance, accountability, and light.

1. Which phrases from the song hit close to home for you? Explain.

❏ My illusion has been shattered
❏ Secrets out—now the healing can begin
❏ Out of the shame, out of the chains
❏ Take the veil of darkness from my eyes
❏ I've found it's love I've feared
❏ Love can take my heart from where it's been

❏ Thoughts that held me captive
❏ Hope that I'm forgiven
❏ There's going to be a cost
❏ Unrelenting guilt
❏ The path I'm on will change my life
❏ Other: _____

Most of us want to deny that we have an addiction, that we've fallen into a trap that's trying to pull us down and eventually take us out. Sexual addiction is not defined by frequency and intensity like revenue on a business spreadsheet. The definition of sexual addiction does not depend on the number of partners but on *why* addicts practice the sexual behavior and *whether they can stop the behavior*. We can even use sex with our spouses to escape intimacy rather than to express intimacy. *The key question is whether sex is an escape from intimacy or an expression of it.*

WILDLY INTIMATE, WILDLY FREE

Remember how salt water is temporarily satisfying to a thirsty man? Pornography is the same way—exhilarating in the moment like a drug high. For many men, porn is their drug of choice, and they find the arousal effective, at least temporarily, in getting the blood pumping, the pulse racing, and the adrenaline flowing, all of which can temporarily ...

- Provide a lift from depression
- Calm frustration
- Ease anger
- Overcome lethargy

- Soothe anxiety
- Combat boredom
- Distract from loneliness
- Suppress low self-esteem

2. Which of these temporary needs or effects fit strongly with your life and situation?

Pornography and other sex addictions are also like salt water in the way they do not satisfy you. In fact, when the drug effect wears off immediately after climax, arousal is replaced by shame, and prowess is replaced by feelings of emptiness. The drug doesn't just wear off, it retaliates!

3. Pornography's drug-like effect also gives us clues about when we are vulnerable to using it for relief. What feelings or conditions do you recognize as making you particularly susceptible?

❏ When I'm depressed   ❏ When I'm anxious or uptight
❏ When I'm frustrated   ❏ When I'm bored
❏ When I'm angry   ❏ When I feel lonely or abandoned
❏ When I feel lethargic   ❏ When I feel down on myself
❏ Other: _____

4. What's behind our desire for and attraction to pornography and other destructive sexual activities? Which of the following most resonates with you? It will take courage to be honest with the others here.

❏ Excitement—pornography can feel wild and dangerous
❏ Pleasure—physical arousal, stimulation, and release
❏ Adventure—porn offers to take you somewhere you haven't been before with a willing companion you've never met
❏ Comfort—temporary escape from the tough times of life

Pornography introduces me to ...

❏ Attractive women who do not hide their bodies
❏ Women who are sexually uninhibited
❏ Women who don't ask questions or make demands
❏ Women who would seemingly do whatever I would want
❏ Women who smile and seem to be both nurturing and erotic
❏ Women I can satisfy
❏ Erotic couples that let me watch and vicariously participate
❏ Other: _____

One counselee's insightful confession is worth noting: "Pornography lets me be both wildly intimate and wildly free at the same time. My fantasy self and my fantasy partner hold nothing back from each other. For me, married sex barely displaces the sheets, and it seems tame, predictable, even mechanical ... like an obligatory act by two domesticated lovers on auto-pilot." *Wildly intimate and wildly free* is how we want to live.

WILDLY INTIMATE: More than just being sexual, this man understands that there is within himself a deep desire to know and be known.

WILDLY FREE. There's something in a man that resists being tamed, that thirsts for adventure, danger, challenge, risk, and conquest. John Eldredge, author of *Wild At Heart*, has noted our attraction to the film roles of cowboys, warriors, soldiers, gladiators, and other heroes. Men line up for films like *Braveheart*, *Gladiator*, *Star Wars*, *Lord of the Rings*, *Saving Private Ryan*. All these fictional characters strike a nerve, exposing contemporary men's desire to do something more masculine and wild than mow the lawn and carry out the trash. It all boils down to understanding what you're really thirsty for and going for the "living water" from Jesus, the Author of intimacy and adventure.

LEADER: If time allows continue on with questions 5 and 6 to prepare the members for their "Taking it Home" assignments this week. Otherwise, move toward closing your time together in a supportive way.

---

5. Can you relate to the concepts of "wildly intimate" and "wildly free"? How do pornography and other sexual activities offer to fulfill our deep desire to be free and wild?

6. What's the problem with porn's pledge to make you feel wildly intimate? Wildly free?

Let's pray that each of us would understand our needs to be wildly intimate and wildly free. How can we pray for you now as you battle to renew your heart and mind? What practical support or accountability needs can this group help you with this next week?

MY PRAYER AND SUPPORT NEEDS:

MY GROUP'S PRAYER AND SUPPORT NEEDS:

TAKING IT HOME

In engaging these next two questions, the more specific you can be, the better. Writing your answers down is an act of honesty, courage, and a profound step toward freedom.

QUESTIONS TO TAKE TO MY HEART

The following questions ask you to look into your heart and consider with brutal honesty your deepest feelings and beliefs. Consider everything you've learned in this study so far. Remember, our behaviors are the best indicator of what we truly believe in our innermost being (Psalm 51:6). Be sure to journal your thoughts, struggles, and insights.

* What old, well-worn patterns of behavior and distorted ways of thinking need to be scraped off? Where do I live in secrets, shame, and shadows?

* What are some subtle lies that I first must identify and renounce? What is the new thinking, the new truths that I need to apply to replace the old?

Questions to Take to God

When you ask God a question, expect His Spirit to respond to your heart and spirit. Be careful not to rush it or manufacture an answer. Don't write down what you think the "right answer" is. Don't turn the Bible into a reference book or spiritual encyclopedia. Just pose your question to God and wait on Him to answer. The litmus test for anything we hear from God is alignment with the Bible as our ultimate source of truth. Focus on listening to God, and record what you hear and sense He is saying to you.

✳ God, what false beliefs do I silently rehearse about myself? About my past?

✳ What false beliefs do I carry deep inside regarding how You feel about me?

✳ Lord, what do you want to tell me about Your relationship with me?

Journal Exercise

Use the journal space on page 48 to capture the false beliefs you've harbored. Make a header "LIES" and write these in a column down the left side of the page. Create another column on the right side of page labeled "TRUTHS." As God reveals lies and corresponding truths, list them here. Review the list often, and continue to denounce and replace the lies with truth.

1 Henry T. Blackaby and Claude V. King, *Experiencing God Workbook*
   (Nashville: LifeWay Press, 1990.)

Renewing the Inside Journal

HOW CAN I BREAK THE CYCLE?

BREAKING THE ICE – 15 MINUTES

In our first three sessions we've wrestled with the questions: What's at stake? Do I want to get well? and What am I thirsty for? The next two sessions are closely connected to each other as we focus on breaking the cycle of acting out. Although inner healing is the key to lasting change, we must break the cycle so we can focus on healing.

LEADER INSTRUCTIONS FOR THE GROUP EXPERIENCE: Have a TV/DVD player set up. Read the following introduction to the group, then play a clip from the DreamWorks™ film Gladiator, *starring Russell Crowe as Maximus. Show the core of Chapter 15, "The Battle of Carthage" (1:23:45 to 1:28:25 minutes on the Standard DVD timer; 1:30:40 to 1:34:16 minutes on the Extended Edition DVD). Note:* Gladiator *contains scenes with intense, graphic violence. After showing the clip, discuss the following questions.*

SURVIVAL

Gladiator is set in ancient Rome. A Roman general named Maximus has been betrayed and sold into slavery and now is returning to Rome as a gladiator forced to provide vile entertainment for the citizens and the emperor, who is re-creating scenes from great Roman military victories. Maximus and the other gladiators are led into the Coliseum to represent the barbarian horde butchered in the Second Fall of Carthage. Let's watch the strategy Maximus uses to survive the deadly onslaught.

1. Maximus is a seasoned man of battle and knows the strategies for survival. What strategy did he employ as he faced the overwhelming enemy? Which men didn't survive?

2. Maximus called out, "Whatever comes out of these gates, we've got a better chance of survival if we work together." What's the value in working together against a dangerous and cunning enemy?

3. When you hear the word "accountability" what comes to mind? If you think of the gladiators being "accountable" for one another's lives, how does that change your perception of accountability?

4. As you reflected on patterns of behavior and distorted beliefs that you need to dump, what key discoveries did you make? What did you hear from God about false beliefs that have become embedded in your heart?

OPENING PRAYER

Although we don't often see it this way God, our world is a brutal and dangerous place. It's far more dangerous in the spiritual realm than on a physical level. You liken the devil to a "roaring lion, looking for anyone he can devour" (1 Peter 5:8). We've each tried battling on our own and in our own strength. Far too often we've fallen in the heat of the battle. Everything within us resists calling out for help, but too much is at stake. Help us as we learn to stand together, cover one another's backs, and see victories won in Your divine power.

OBJECTIVES FOR THIS SESSION

- Understand the three building-block behaviors of sex addiction
- Learn 4 of 10 practical principles for breaking the cycle through accountability
- Realize that our survival and victory hinge upon being connected with men who are accountable for one another
- Gain a proper understanding of accountability
- Accept the priority of stopping destructive sexual behaviors

Discovering the Truth – 40 minutes

In our last session, we focused on understanding for what we really thirst. Our focus in Session 4 will be breaking the cycle of addictive behavior through accountability.

DO I WANT TO GET WELL?
WHAT AM I THIRSTY FOR?
HOW CAN I BREAK THE CYCLE?

How will I counterattack?
What are my deepest longings?
Am I willing to embrace my pain?
What will be my legacy?

Building-Block Behaviors

There are three key building-block behaviors common to all sex addictions. These three are often developed early in life and form the foundation upon which other sexual behaviors are built. The key building-block behaviors are:

- Sexual fantasizing
- Use of pornography in all forms
- Masturbation

1. How do you see these three behaviors interrelating and fueling one another? Why do you think these three behaviors are so destructive?

2. What longings do you think men might be trying to satisfy as they engage in fantasy, porn, and masturbation? Why might these behaviors have such strong draw for us?

For the sex addict, fantasy is created by a need to satisfy deep emotional or spiritual longings. At the same time, we view sex as the solution to the need for love, touch, nurture, and affirmation. Pornography escalates the intensity of the fantasy to higher and higher levels of lust. Masturbation is the physical expression of the lust and fills some needs for touch, nurture, and ecstasy.

The drawing power and addictive nature are increased by several factors:

- *A High*—Fantasizing alone is exciting enough to produce adrenaline and other chemical changes in the pleasure centers of the brain.
- *Escape*—Because of the positive mood-altering effects of these behaviors, they provide escape from unpleasant emotions and reduce stress.
- *Panacea*—These sexual activities are used in an attempt to heal loneliness, boredom, and unmet needs in imaginary ways.
- *Easy*—Fantasy partners are perfect—totally caring, attractive, perfectly nurturing, and completely sexual. They require nothing from us, or so it seems.
- *Triggers*—Even ordinary things can trigger an individual's fantasy life, and thereby be pornographic for him.
- *Embedded*—Masturbation can become deeply embedded in childhood and for some it becomes the only escape from painful family chaos.
- *Satisfaction*—As with any addiction, these behaviors continue to seduce us by temporarily satisfying some needs in a superficial way, but they never satisfy the emotional and spiritual thirst deep within our souls.

STEPS FOR BREAKING THE CYCLE

As we begin to turn to Jesus with our deepest thirsts, there are 10 practical steps from the Book of Nehemiah that can help us overcome destructive habits or addictions and begin to replace them with real freedom and hope. In this session, we'll discuss the first four.

LEADER: *Ask various group members to read the Scripture verses. Discuss as many discovery questions as time permits. This "Discovering the Truth" provides four key steps in breaking the cycle of acting out. Try to keep the discussion moving. It will help to highlight in advance the questions you don't want to miss. By the end of the session, be sure the group members understand the urgency of stopping sexual behaviors, and vital role of accountability to make this happen.*

Step 1: Identify Losses and Begin to Grieve with God

Because of their overt disobedience to God, Israel had been in captivity in Persia for 70 years. Nehemiah was an Israelite slave but was in an influential role as the trusted cupbearer of King Artaxerxes. God used this leader to teach us valuable lessons about overcoming what seems like an impossible task.

² Hanani, one of my brothers, arrived with men from Judah, and I questioned them about Jerusalem and the Jewish remnant that had returned from exile. ³ They said to me, "The survivors in the province, who returned from the exile, are in great trouble and disgrace. Jerusalem's wall has been broken down, and its gates have been burned down."

⁴ When I heard these words, I sat down and wept. I mourned for a number of days, fasting and praying before the God of heaven. ⁵ I said, "Lord God of heaven, the great and awe-inspiring God who keeps His gracious covenant with those who love Him and keep His commands.

NEHEMIAH 1:2-5, HCSB

3. How did Nehemiah respond to the new about the devastation in Jerusalem? Why would grieving past hurts, losses ,and missed opportunities be such an important place to begin the process of healing?

4. What attitude(s) did Nehemiah exhibit through his prayer in verse 5? In what ways does Nehemiah's approach of sorrow, humility, and brokenness contrast with that of strong leaders that typically come to mind?

When Nehemiah first heard about the destruction of Jerusalem you might expect that he'd stand boldly and with rugged individualism engage in a great plan to conquer the problem. A successful recovery from porn and sex addiction begins with humility and sorrow. In humility we admit that we can't control our own lives and must rely on God's help. Sorrow helps us begin to identify and process our losses and hurts of the past so these don't sabotage the healing process and drive us back into addiction. This process is like peeling the layers of an onion and so can take time to work through.

Step 2: Take Responsibility

From a starting point of humility, Nehemiah continued with an sincere and enlightening two-part prayer.

> *⁶ Let Your eyes be open and Your ears be attentive to hear Your servant's prayer that I now pray to You day and night for Your servants, the Israelites. I confess the sins we have committed against You. Both I and my father's house have sinned. ⁷ We have acted corruptly toward You and have not kept the commands, statutes, and ordinances You gave Your servant Moses. ⁸ Please remember what You commanded Your servant Moses: "If you are unfaithful, I will scatter you among the peoples. ⁹ But if you return to Me and carefully observe My commands, even though your exiles were banished to the ends of the earth, I will gather them from there and bring them to the place where I chose to have My name dwell." ¹⁰ They are Your servants and Your people. You redeemed them by Your great power and strong hand.*
>
> NEHEMIAH 1:6-10, HCSB

5. How did Nehemiah take responsibility for his failures? Why is the second part of his prayer in verses 9-10, where he expresses a heartfelt desire to change, so important to returning home?

Once we confess, we must also take the next step as Nehemiah did: He expressed a heartfelt willingness to repent—to change the course of his life—and return home. Grief over the pain and losses of sexual addiction leads to a willingness to confess our failure to obey God's commands. Our journey begins when we honestly admit the condition of our lives rather than denying the truth or blaming others.

Step 3: Don't Cover Up

> *² So the king asked me, "Why are you looking so sad? You don't look sick to me. You must be deeply troubled." Then I was terrified, ³ but I replied, "Long live the king! How can I not be sad? For the city where my ancestors are buried is in ruins, and the gates have been destroyed by fire." ⁴ The king asked, "Well, how can I help you?" With a prayer to the God of heaven, ⁵ I replied, "If it please the king, and if you are pleased with me, your servant, send me to Judah to rebuild the city where my ancestors are buried." ⁶ The king, with the queen sitting beside him, asked, "How long will you be gone? When will you return?" After I told him how long I would be gone, the king agreed to my request.*
>
> NEHEMIAH 2:2-6, NLT

6. What was Nehemiah's attitude when the king asked him to share his difficult feelings and his needs (verses 2 and 4)? How have you typically responded to others when you were hurting, troubled, or needed help?

¹⁵ *The prayer of faith will save the sick person, and the Lord will raise him up; and if he has committed sins, he will be forgiven.* ¹⁶ *Therefore, confess your sins to one another and pray for one another, so that you may be healed. The intense prayer of the righteous is very powerful.*

JAMES 5:15-16, HCSB

7. Why is it difficult to open up and reveal our feelings, needs, and struggles to others? According to James 5:15-16, what's the payoff of developing a small group of people we can trust and with whom we can be real?

Honestly expressing emotions and needs is one of the most difficult things for addicts, especially the male variety. Many spend a lifetime in self-destructive behaviors to avoid being vulnerable. Healing from sexual addiction means we must resist the temptation to cover up. It takes courage to be honest with yourself, God, and others you can trust about what's really going on inside.

STEP 4: ENLIST SUPPORT

Because of Nehemiah's prayers the king not only allowed Nehemiah to go to Jerusalem to rebuild the city wall, he also provided him with letters for safe passage and the material needed for the reconstruction. But it didn't stop there ...

⁹ *I went to the governors of the region west of the Euphrates and gave them the king's letters. The king had also sent officers of the infantry and cavalry with me.* ¹⁰ *When Sanballat the Horonite and Tobiah the Ammonite official heard that someone had come to seek the well-being of the Israelites, they were greatly displeased.* ¹¹ *After I arrived in Jerusalem and had been there three days,* ¹² *I got up at night and took a few men with me. I didn't tell anyone what my God had laid on my heart to do for Jerusalem. The only animal I took was the one I was riding.*

NEHEMIAH 2:9-12, HCSB

8. What might have happened if Nehemiah had taken this long journey through enemy territory alone? In our journey to recovery and healing, when might we need an army with us (verse 9)? When might we need those trusted "few men" (verse 12)?

God never intended for us to struggle alone. We need each other; we were designed for strong relationships. Check this out:

⁹ Two people are better off than one, for they can help each other succeed. ¹⁰ If one person falls, the other can reach out and help. But someone who falls alone is in real trouble. ... ¹² A person standing alone can be attacked and defeated, but two can stand back-to-back and conquer. Three are even better, for a triple-braided cord is not easily broken.

ECCLESIASTES 4:9-10,12, NLT

9. In what ways do the benefits of standing together remind you of the scene we watched from *Gladiator*? What are some ways we can stand together to support one another in the battle we're fighting.

It is very rare, if not impossible, for a person to heal from sexual addiction alone. When we're under attack by the Enemy, we need people who will hold us accountable. We need a ready list of names and phone numbers for people in our 24/7 group.

EMBRACING THE TRUTH – 15 MINUTES

LEADER: *This section focuses on helping group members integrate what they've learned from the story of Nehemiah into their own hearts and lives. Be sure that group members leave with a good understanding of the process of sexual acting out.*

Just as in *Gladiator* or the story of Nehemiah, battling pornography and other sex addictions requires patience, determination, and pushing through dark, difficult times. We must embrace the spirit of warriors, execute a strong plan, focus on getting well, and stand together helping one another to thwart the attacks of the Enemy. *There's a direct correlation between how much work people invest in recovery and how permanent their recovery becomes.*

Identify your losses and begin to grieve with God ... Take responsibility ... Don't cover up ... Enlist support

1. In which of these four areas do you most struggle? What steps do you need to take? How can this group can encourage and support you?

2. How many people do you currently have in your life who will struggle alongside you on your journey to healing, purity, and integrity? Describe the level of openness and trust in your relationships.

3. Does your wife (or girlfriend) have a clue about any of your struggles with past wounds or with sexual temptation? Discuss approaches to opening these discussions with a spouse in ways that gain support rather than causing shock and alarm.

A 90-day abstinence contract is one tool that has been successful in reversing the level of neuro-chemical tolerance addicts have built up in their brains. A period of abstinence also reverses an addict's core false belief that "Sex is my most important need." For married men, this is another way to enlist the support of their wives. Either way, an abstinence contract should be considered only with the guidance of a qualified therapist.

ANATOMY OF ACTING OUT

Many people say that they just suddenly fell into temptation, but it's seldom that simple. If we're honest, we realize that we plan and determine to act out well before the event. While the specifics vary with each person, the basic anatomy of acting out includes five components:

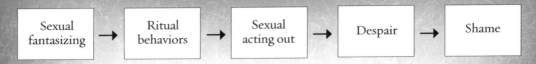

| Sexual fantasizing | → | Ritual behaviors | → | Sexual acting out | → | Despair | → | Shame |

In order to halt the progression toward acting out, it's critical to focus on the behaviors that lead up to and set the stage for acting out. Sexual fantasies are almost always symbolic of deep wounds and unmet needs. We'll return to this topic in Sessions 6 and 7.

Stopping ritual behaviors is the other key to stopping destructive sexual behaviors. If an alcoholic goes to a bar he'll likely take a drink. Rituals include all the thoughts and actions that lead up to the event, whether simple or elaborate. Some examples of rituals might be: surfing the Internet or cable TV when alone, masturbating, viewing pornography, driving into certain neighborhoods, getting cash from the ATM, visiting a massage parlor or bookstore, and building relationships that lead to sexual encounters.

4. When we find ourselves approaching any rituals, we must recognize how destructive they are. What roadblocks or boundaries could we establish in advance to prevent these rituals?

5. What healthy rituals could we discipline ourselves to implement in place of our sexual rituals? Consider activities that foster physical, emotional, spiritual, and especially relational health.

Battling to stop sexual rituals and acting out is never easy. Discipline and strong determination are required. You must settle the question, "Do I really want to get well?" Then you'll need all 10 steps we're discovering from the story of Nehemiah.

CONNECTING — 20 MINUTES

LEADER: *The group should be starting to gel now. Use this "Connecting" time to help group members see this group as a band of brothers—a group that can work together to fight whatever comes at them.*

Most people resist the idea of accountability. We don't welcome the idea of opening up our lives to someone else. But accountability is an integral part of the healing journey. *In fact, your recovery and healing are dependent on your willingness to make yourself accountable to other "safe" people in your life.* This is especially true during the early months of recovery. Safe people are those with whom you can be totally honest and not fear damage to your relationship with those people nor public exposure. Proverbs 12:15 reminds us that "Fools are headstrong and do what they like; wise people take advice" (The Message).

What exactly does "being accountable" mean? If you're accountable with your money, you show how you spend it. Being accountable in sexuality and relationships means being honest about yourself and pursuing change through the powerful influence and support of authentic relationships. We need others on the healing journey willing to share our struggles, thoughts, success, hurts, fears, and desires. By opening up, we break the power of secrecy, shame, and shadows so we can continue to move toward sexual integrity.

Heart Writing

> *LEADER: Lead the group in a writing exercise. Be sure to bring pens or pencils to pass around. Encourage the men to make the most of this exercise by being as honest as possible with themselves and with God.*
>
> - *Allow this experience some time; don't rush it.*
> - *Put on quiet background music (You may purchase the CD* Pursued by God: Redemptive Worship *from Serendipity House, or select your own music.)*
> - *Help each person create his own personal space. This is not a time to chat; make it very honoring.*
> - *Trust God to speak to each person individually through this exercise.*
> - *After allowing 10 minutes to write, invite group members to read their prayers aloud.*

Take 10 minutes and use the space on the next page to write a brief prayer to God.

(1) Tell God how you feel about yourself and your current emotions connected with sexual temptations (sad, glad, angry, hurt, lonely, fear, guilt, shame). Try to explain why you're feeling those emotions..

(2) Share regrets about choices you've made and the resulting problems these caused.

(3) Confess the destructive patterns of behavior in your life, and ask God to help you develop a plan for eliminating these and keeping them out of your life.

(4) Ask God to give you the boldness to lock arms with at least two other men (within or outside this group), and for the courage to continue to keep fighting.

My Prayer to God ...

Spend a few minutes allowing each person who wants to read his prayer or seek prayers from the group or to encourage others. What practical support or accountability needs can this group help you with this next week?

MY PRAYER & SUPPORT NEEDS:

MY GROUP'S PRAYER & SUPPORT NEEDS:

LEADER: Close by praying for God to help each person to connect with at least two godly, safe people with whom they can lock arms as accountability partners. Let the men know that you'll be asking at the next meeting for each person to identify his small accountability group.

TAKING IT HOME

In engaging these next two questions, the more specific you can be, the better. Writing your answers down is an act of courageous honesty and a profound step toward freedom.

QUESTIONS TO TAKE TO MY HEART

The following questions ask you to look into your heart and consider your deepest hurts and disappointments. Remember, if you don't allow yourself to grieve your pain and losses from the past then these wounds will likely sabotage your healing process at some point. Jesus Himself confirms the importance of grieving in Matthew 5:4: "Blessed are those who mourn, because they will be comforted."

✳ What are some key losses, traumatic events, abuse, and neglect in my life that I need to grieve? What events in my story have really hurt me?

✳ I know I'm blinded to some of my ritual behaviors that lead up to acting out. In my last episode, what thoughts and behaviors preceded my acting out?

✳ Which behaviors am I still resistant to release or eliminate from my life? What drives that resistance? What desires am I trying to satisfy through those behaviors?

JOURNAL EXERCISE

Use the journal space on page 62 to begin listing the losses and painful events from your past. After each loss, jot down how you currently feel about that loss. Review the list often, add to it, and continue to grieve as you ask God to redeem your life from the hurts.

Losses to Grieve Journal

HOW WILL I COUNTERATTACK?

BREAKING THE ICE – 15 MINUTES

EVERY MAN'S BATTLE

God designed sex as a way for a husband and wife to experience oneness and express intimacy. He even created the idea of arousal as a part of that intimacy in marriage. We all have sexual triggers that we must recognize and control, especially those triggers that draw us toward inappropriate or potentially harmful behaviors. There are two types of triggers: *external* (visual, auditory, touch, smell, taste) and *internal* (feelings/emotions, memories, situations, etc.).

1. Recall a recent trip to the mall. Envision the usual activity in the food court, a music store, a trendy clothing store, and a bookstore. What possible triggers might we experience while shopping at the mall?

As we discussed in Session 1, sexual temptation has been a prime enemy weapon from the beginning. Men tend to be visually stimulated and are particularly vulnerable to external stimuli, but internal memories and fantasies are powerful as well. Listen together to the song "Every Man's Battle."

LEADER INSTRUCTIONS FOR THE GROUP EXPERIENCE: *Page 4 shows a companion music CD called* Somebody's Daughter *available from Serendipity House. Have a CD player queued up to play the song "Every Man's Battle—Remix" from that CD. If you like, you can download lyrics from* www.SerendipityHouse.com/Community *(under Group Leaders - Leadership Aids). Ask group members to close their eyes and listen with their hearts open. At the end of the song, discuss the following questions.*

2. Do you think it's accurate to say that every man battles with lust and other sexual issues? What messages from the song grabbed your heart?

3. This song lays out several steps for fighting the battle of lust, pornography, and other sex addictions. Which of these would you most want to be true in your life? Explain.

- ❐ "Live out in the open"
- ❐ "Confess our deepest secrets"
- ❐ "Hold every single thought captive"
- ❐ "Redirect our eyes"
- ❐ "Brothers on our guard"
- ❐ "Stand each other's ground"
- ❐ "Break our darkest habits"
- ❐ "Encourage one another"
- ❐ "Minds and hearts vigilant"

4. As you approached your questions to take to your heart this week, what losses did you identify? Were you able to begin to let yourself feel grief? Explain.

OPENING PRAYER

God, we're fully aware that there's a battle raging inside us for our hearts, our allegiance, our legacies, and our destinies. The worst part is that we find ourselves at times joining forces with the Enemy. We find ourselves falling back into old patterns of thought and behavior. Too often when the attacks come, they catch us off-guard in moments of weakness. Help us to see the Enemy in all its foul destruction. And help us catch a vision today of advance preparation, divine power, and winning this war.

OBJECTIVES FOR THIS SESSION

- Understand the remaining 6 of 10 practical principles for breaking the cycle through accountability
- Recognize key symptoms of sexual addiction
- Accept the vital role of advance preparation before temptations hit
- Learn to augment our strong defense against attacks with strong life rebuilding efforts
- Find motivations to keep fighting and rebuilding
- Begin to develop an accountability plan

Discovering the Truth – 30 minutes

DO I WANT TO GET WELL?
WHAT AM I THIRSTY FOR?
HOW CAN I BREAK THE CYCLE?
HOW WILL I COUNTERATTACK?

What are my deepest longings?
Am I willing to embrace my pain?
What will be my legacy?

In this session, we'll continue discussing the topics of accountability and breaking the cycle of sexual behavior. As we continue to look at Nehemiah's example, we'll consider six additional principles for breaking free and guarding our freedom. It's not enough to want freedom; we must take action by developing an accountability plan before temptation strikes.

STEP 5: GO FOR IT ... ONE DAY AT A TIME

When Nehemiah surveyed the damage in the city, it must have looked like a war zone or a city hit by a tsunami or hurricane. Many would have given up discouraged and disillusioned, but Nehemiah was going for it!

[18] *I told them how the gracious hand of my God had been on me, and what the king had said to me.*

They said, "Let's start rebuilding," and they were encouraged to do this good work. [19] *When Sanballat the Horonite, Tobiah the Ammonite official, and Geshem the Arab heard about this, they mocked and despised us, and said, "What is this you're doing? Are you rebelling against the king?"*

[20] *I gave them this reply, "The God of heaven is the One who will grant us success. We, His servants, will start building, but you have no share, right, or historic claim in Jerusalem."*

NEHEMIAH 2:18-20, HCSB

1. Apart from his own deep desire to rebuild the city, what two other sources (see verses 18 and 20) gave Nehemiah confidence to press on as he faced an enormous task, criticism, and ridicule?

No one was overwhelmed or discouraged by the enormity of the project because Nehemiah's plan was to rebuild the wall around the city one small section at a time. He wasn't focused on the short-term failures, but on the long-term goal of restoration. If we try to fix everything in our lives at once, we'll become discouraged and give up. We are wise to heed the advice of Alcoholics Anonymous that says, "One day at a time" as we tackle just today and just one thing at a time.

STEP 6: DUMP THE GARBAGE

We all like to envision rebuilding great cities and winning battles as glorious endeavors, but in truth they're dirty, gritty, difficult, long-haul efforts. It's tempting to hide or ignore the filthy areas of life, but Israel did just the opposite. When Nehemiah refers to the Dung Gate, he's not using a clever phrase. This was literally the gate through which garbage and dung were hauled out of the city and burned. Although there were several other gates (Sheep, Fish, Horse, Water, Old, East, Fountain, and Inspection gates), the Dung Gate was highlighted in the plan, the rebuilding process, and also the celebration when the restoration was completed.

²:¹³ I [Nehemiah] went out at night through the Valley Gate toward the Serpent's Well and the Dung Gate, and I inspected the walls of Jerusalem that had been broken down and its gates that had been destroyed by fire. ... ³:¹⁴ Malchijah son of Rechab, ruler over the district of Beth-haccherem, repaired the Dung Gate. He rebuilt it and installed its doors, bolts, and bars. ... ¹²:³¹ Then I brought the leaders of Judah up on top of the wall, and I appointed two large processions that gave thanks. One went to the right on the wall, toward the Dung Gate.

NEHEMIAH 2:13; 3:14; 12:31, HCSB

2. Why do you think the Dung Gate assignment might be one of the most important in rebuilding a city? In rebuilding our lives?

A city that can't get rid of its waste chokes on its own garbage; the whole city carries stench and disease. The Apostle Paul helped many men deal with the garbage in their lives and offers this advice:

> ¹² *The night is almost gone, and the day is near. Therefore let us lay aside the deeds of darkness and put on the armor of light.* ¹³ *Let us behave properly as in the day, not in carousing and drunkenness, not in sexual promiscuity and sensuality, not in strife and jealousy.* ¹⁴ *But put on the Lord Jesus Christ, and make no provision for the flesh in regard to its lusts.*
>
> ROMANS 13:12-14, NASB

3. What is Paul's strategy in Romans 13 for dealing with the garbage in our lives—the "deeds of darkness," "the flesh," and our distorted desires or "lusts"? Identify some specific kinds of sexual garbage we need to dump and "make no provision for."

Dumping the garbage could mean getting rid of your ability to access the Internet by installing a filter and accountability software. It could mean canceling your cable or satellite television. It might mean getting rid of a secret post office box, bank account, affair partner, or even a friendship that could lead you into trouble.

Just as importantly, you need to get rid of the garbage of negative thoughts, feelings of shame, painful memories, unresolved anger, resentment, blame, denial, and anxiety that can trip you up on the path to healing.

STEP 7: REBUILD CLOSE TO HOME FIRST

As Nehemiah tried to motivate the people to persevere in the rebuilding process and to give their best effort to creating a strong wall, he implemented an ingenious strategy.

> ¹⁰ *After them Jedaiah son of Harumaph made repairs across from his house. Next to him Hattush the son of Hashabneiah made repairs.* ... ²¹ *Beside him Meremoth son of Uriah, son of Hakkoz, made repairs to another section, from the door of Eliashib's house to the end of his house.* ... ²³ *After them Benjamin and Hasshub made repairs opposite their house. Beside them Azariah son of Maaseiah, son of Ananiah, made repairs beside his house.* ... ²⁹ *After them Zadok son of Immer made repairs opposite his house. And beside him Shemaiah son of Shecaniah, guard of the East Gate, made repairs.*
>
> NEHEMIAH 3:10,21,23,29, HCSB

4. Why would rebuilding around their own homes provide incentive and motivation? In practical terms, how can we employ this strategy in our own lives?

So many people who begin the road to recovery get ahead of themselves. They want to jump immediately into helping others. This will come eventually, but put first things first. In the beginning, keep your focus on saving yourself and your own family.

Step 8: Prepare for Weakness in Times of Strength

8 [The enemies] all plotted together to come and fight against Jerusalem and throw it into confusion. 9 So we prayed to our God and stationed a guard because of them day and night. ... 13 So I stationed people behind the lowest sections of the wall, at the vulnerable areas. I stationed them by families with their swords, spears, and bows.

Nehemiah 4:8-9,13, hcsb

5. How and on which areas did Nehemiah focus with the certain knowledge that an attack was coming? Why is preparing in advance of attacks so critical?

The message for breaking free with accountability is clear: you cannot wait for the attack to come. The Enemy will tempt us at the weakest places in our defenses. Most of us think, *When I'm tempted, I'll call someone.* Here's the problem: part of the temptation is that we won't want to call anyone. It's critical to have a clearly defined plan in place so that when the attack comes, we'll be ready.

Step 9: Balance Offense and Defense in the Battle

15 When our enemies realized that we knew their scheme and that God had frustrated it, every one of us returned to his own work on the wall. 16 From that day on, half of my men did the work while the other half held spears, shields, bows, and armor. The officers supported all the people of Judah, 17 who were rebuilding the wall. The laborers who carried the loads worked with one hand and held a weapon with the other. 18 Each of the builders had his sword strapped around his waist while he was building, and the trumpeter was beside me.

Nehemiah 4:15-18, hcsb

6. In what ways did Nehemiah balance defensive protection and offensive rebuilding? What would have happened in the end without defense? Without offense?

Rebuilding alone leaves us vulnerable to attacks that will sabotage healing. Defense alone is negative and eventually results in discouragement. We must build into our lives new behaviors, transformed beliefs and attitudes, restored and deeper relationships, and new and deeper ways to connect to God and others. We need to be just as accountable to do rebuilding as we are to refraining from the sins we hate.

STEP 10: FIND MOTIVATION TO KEEP FIGHTING

[14] After I made an inspection, I stood up and said to the nobles, the officials, and the rest of the people, "Don't be afraid of them. Remember the great and awe-inspiring LORD, and fight for your countrymen, your sons and daughters, your wives and homes." ... [20] Wherever you hear the trumpet sound, rally to us there. Our God will fight for us!"

NEHEMIAH 4:14,20, HCSB

7. What motivations did Nehemiah lay out for the people so they would persevere in rebuilding and in fighting?

If we're motivated by self-oriented fears, then we won't get very far. However, if we remain mindful of those we really love, we'll focus on how our healing is also for them. As we realize the depth of pain we've caused family, friends, and God, then we can be motivated by a loving desire never to hurt them again.

EMBRACING THE TRUTH – 25 MINUTES

> LEADER: *This section focuses on helping group members integrate lessons from Nehemiah into their own hearts and lives.* NOTE: *Depending on your remaining time and the needs of your group, you may choose to review the descriptions for each of the 11 symptoms or simply mention each one.*

SYMPTOMS OF SEX ADDICTION

Preoccupation with Sexual Behaviors — These are connected to a strong fantasy life. Eventually, sex becomes the central organizing principle of a person's life. Occupational, social, family, professional, and legal difficulties are the natural outcome.

Escalating Patterns of Sexual Behavior — The acting out always worsens over the long haul, even if there are extended periods with no acting out.

Acting Distant or Withdrawn — Withdrawal stems from preoccupation with sex and from feelings of guilt, shame, and fear of getting caught.

Depression and Mood Swings — Alternating from the excitement of the chase in rituals and acting out to the shame and despair that follows, people deny problems or they rage if questioned.

Irritability — To avoid their honest emotions, sex addicts create enormous defense mechanisms. Their own behaviors as well as past abuses take root as deep resentments and anger in the heart.

Abuse of Self or Others — Sex addicts may abuse others if they've been abused in the past. Many abuse themselves.

Resistance to Supervision or Criticism — Resistance is a defense to prevent being challenged.

Use of Sexual Humor —Sex addicts see sexual humor in most situations. Sexual jokes can be used to gauge another's reaction, and to recruit a new partner if that reaction is favorable.

Inappropriate Sexual Behavior or Overt Sexual Advances — These occur inside as well as outside the marriage bed, and result when sex addicts experience increasing frustration with sex in marriage that they can't articulate.

Indicators from Intuition — Although sex addicts struggle with intimacy, impressions about things not adding up well should be heeded.

Direct Evidence — This is the most obvious symptom but often the last to surface.

1. Identify two of the above symptoms you believe are most true for you. What personal issues or beliefs do you think lie behind or cause these behaviors?

COUNTERATTACK PLANS

At the end of this session, we'll discuss a scene from the World War II film *Saving Private Ryan*. Recovery from porn or other sex addictions is a lot like fighting a war. Standing together—accountability—is a vital part of winning this war. A lone ranger will not win a war against a powerful enemy. We each need a healthy support group that encourages total and rigorous honesty, vulnerability, confession, acts of restitution, accountability, and deepening relationships with Jesus, family, and friends.

Be sober! Be on the alert! Your adversary the Devil is prowling around like a roaring lion, looking for anyone he can devour.

1 PETER 5:8, HCSB

2. According to 1 Peter 5:8, will we ever be free from temptation and the need to fight to retain our freedom from addiction? What practical changes do we need to make as we recognize this ruthless battle is raging?

3. From your past experience and the truths we've studied, what practical preparations can help us when the temptation and enemy attacks are strong?

To break the cycle of sexual acting out and to prepare for attacks, we must focus on the fantasizing and rituals that lead up to the sexual acts. Once we engage in the rituals, it's very difficult to turn back. While we need to stop the behaviors, we must focus on our hearts and minds.

Above all else, guard your heart, for it is the wellspring of life.

PROVERBS 4:23, NIV

4. What do you think we can do to guard our hearts? What are some ways we can stay connected with our hearts, with our accountability groups, and with God?

24 Let us consider how we spur one another on toward love and good deeds. 25 Let us not give up meeting together, as some are in the habit of doing, but let us encourage one another—all the more as you see the Day approaching.

HEBREWS 10:24-25 NIV

19 My dear friends, if you know people who have wandered off from God's truth, don't write them off. Go after them. 20 Get them back and you will have rescued precious lives from destruction and prevented an epidemic of wandering away from God.

JAMES 5:19-20, THE MESSAGE

5. What are ways we can spur one another on toward love and good deeds?

LEADER: Be sure that each group member has a couple of accountability partners in place. You may need to help make the connections in some cases. In addition, be sure that each group member has Internet filtering and reporting software installed in each of his computers.

---

6. With whom can you or have you developed a "no pretenses" accountability relationship? (First names only please.) Do you have an Internet filter and reporting software on your computers? If so, which software?

To become truly accountable, you have to come to accept the reality of where you are on the journey to healing, and the reality of the brutal battle for your heart, your family, and your life.

NOTE: Some strong Christian Internet filtering and reporting software options include: integrity.com, bsafehome.com, and afafilter.com. Other strong options are: contentwatch.com, cybersitter.com, netnanny.com, and safeeyes.com. Additionally, covenanteyes.com offers free accountability partner accounts.

CONNECTING – 20 MINUTES

TAKING THOUGHTS CAPTIVE

LEADER INSTRUCTIONS FOR THE GROUP EXPERIENCE: Have a TV/DVD player set up. Read the following introduction to the group, and then play a scene from the 1998 award-winning film Saving Private Ryan, *starring Tom Hanks, Edward Burns, and Tom Sizemore. First, show the portion of Chapter 13, "Big Mystery" from 1:37:05 to 1:39:25 minutes on the DVD timer. NOTE: This movie contains graphic violence and coarse language. After showing the first scene, discuss the following questions.*

1. What were the two competing opinions about how to handle the German POW? What factors do you think determined each of the two views?

2. Why was the vocal private so upset about the captain's decision to release their captive?

The platoon we encountered in the first scene later becomes engaged in an all-out battle with the enemy. Pay attention to the enemy soldier without a helmet in this next scene; he should look familiar.

LEADER: Now, show a second scene from Saving Private Ryan. *Skip ahead to Chapter 18, "The Alamo." Show the very end of the scene beginning at 2:32:05 on the DVD timer. Continue into the beginning of Chapter 19, "The Bridge," and stop at the 2:35:05 mark. After showing the second scene, discuss the remaining questions.*

3. Do you think the enemy recalled the captain's earlier mercy toward him? What was the result of sending the captive away in the first scene?

4. Do you think the enemy honored the "order" or "discipline" of war? Explain.

5. What did the soldiers learn about taking captives in a war?

³ *For though we live in the world, we do not wage war as the world does.* ⁴ *The weapons we fight with are not the weapons of the world. On the contrary, they have divine power to demolish strongholds.* ⁵ *We demolish arguments and every pretension that sets itself up against the knowledge of God, and* <u>*we take captive every thought to make it obedient to Christ.*</u>

2 CORINTHIANS 10:3-5, NIV

The war we're engaged in is not a physical war, but a deadly war for our hearts and our legacies. As Christ-followers, we have access to divinely powerful weapons.

6. Thinking about the scenes from *Saving Private Ryan*, how can we avoid simply sending a thought away or avoiding it? What are some ways we can "take captive every thought" *and* "make it obedient to Christ" (verse 5)?

Just as the enemy in the film, our enemy doesn't play by the rules. In the battle over our thoughts, there's no Geneva Convention or code of conduct. Taking every thought captive does not mean trying to send it away, just avoiding it, or guarding your eyes so you never have an "enemy" thought. When you engage an enemy, grab it, tie it down, keep it close, and interrogate it. Find out from the enemy thought what you can about the battles in your heart—your loneliness, isolation, anger, anxiety, or distorted beliefs. Once you've gained all you can from the enemy thought, don't give it another chance!

Taking life one day at a time, dumping the garbage, rebuilding, and maintaining accountability will be the core of your program for the rest of your life. This reality isn't just because you are involved in pornography. It's because you are a man who seeks to follow Christ. God never intended us to plow through the hardships of life on our own. He designed us to live in true community, locking arms with a band of brothers and taking the journey together.

My Prayer Needs:

My Group's Prayer Needs:

LEADER: *Pray for each man in his battle and for the accountability plan that he'll begin this week.*

Taking It Home

As you begin to develop your accountability plan, there will be some hesitation and spiritual resistance. Taking the following questions to your heart and to God should help clear the way.

Questions to Take to My Heart

The following questions ask you to look into your heart and consider with brutal honesty your deepest feelings and beliefs. Consider everything you've learned in this study so far. Remember, our behaviors are the best indicator of what we truly believe in our innermost being (Psalm 51:6). Be sure to journal your thoughts, struggles, and insights.

✳ Which of the 10 steps from Sessions 4 and 5 are twisting my guts? What's really driving my anxiety? What am I afraid will happen? What is it that I'm really trying to hold onto and protect?

A Question to Take to God

When you ask God a question, expect His Spirit to respond to your heart and spirit. Be careful not to rush it or manufacture an answer. Don't write down what you think the "right answer" is. Don't turn the Bible into a reference book or spiritual encyclopedia. Just pose your question to God and wait on Him to answer. The litmus test for anything we hear from God is alignment with the Bible as our ultimate source of truth. Focus on listening to God, and record what you hear and sense He is saying to you.

> ✳ God, you know my heart better than I know it myself. Where am I most vulnerable? What are Your greatest concerns for me?

Journal Exercise

Use the journal space on page 77 to begin developing your accountability plan. Just walk through the steps that follow:

1. Make a list of behaviors, rituals, and triggers you need to shut down. Choose one or two behaviors that you can address immediately. Ask God to help you face these behaviors head on with success.

2. Drawing from the men in the group or other men you trust, ask God to show you three to five men with whom you can feel safe and share your most intimate thoughts, feelings, and behaviors.

3. Once you have connected with three to five men, set up a weekly accountability meeting with these guys.

4. Plan to call accountability partners on a regular basis and check in. Program their phone numbers in your phone so you have easy access.

5. Begin calling your closest support friends daily. This develops a discipline so when you're in crisis, you'll already be accustomed to calling.

6. Make a brief list of questions you would like your accountability partners to ask you. Develop open-ended questions rather than yes/no questions. Get to know what's going on in each other's lives.

7. Purchase a notebook or create a secure file on your computer for a journal. Make daily entries of your feelings, experiences, or prayers that capture where you are in the healing journey.

8. Develop your initial accountability plan, and give a copy to your accountability partners for feedback. Keep updating your plan as new developments take place in your life. Commit your plan to God.

My Accountability Plan

WHAT ARE MY DEEPEST LONGINGS?

BREAKING THE ICE – 15 MINUTES

LEADER: These "Breaking the Ice" questions are intended to help group members begin to awaken some deeper desires of their hearts. Be sure each group member takes a turn answering the questions. If anyone needs more time to come up with a response, you may come back to him.

1. If you discovered Aladdin's magic lamp at a garage sale, what three wishes would you make? Dream big! Discuss.

2. There was a series of beer commercials that ended with the line, "It just doesn't get any better than this!" What one or two activities really make you come alive? Describe to the group a memorable time when "it just couldn't get any better" and how you felt

3. As you thought about it this past week, which of the 10 steps for breaking free is the greatest struggle for you? Deep down, what do you think is really driving your struggle?

4. What have you heard from God about His heart and His concerns for you? In what ways has knowing that God is pulling for you changed your perspective?

OPENING PRAYER

God, we're standing together so each man in this group can break free from the sexual traps into which he's been lured. But we want more than accountability; we want—we need—lasting change. Help us as we begin to unravel more of what's going on inside us. The draw of pornography and sex addictions is that they do give us pleasure, excite us, help us escape, and make us feel alive ... but only for fleeting moments. Clearly, we've believed the lies of sex and bought into false intimacy. Help us find the real thing as we chuck out the counterfeits!

OBJECTIVES FOR THIS SESSION

- Understand that we were created for deep intimacy and even ecstasy
- Discuss the seven root desires of the heart—what men need and long for
- Begin to come to grips with strategic arrows and wounds that have drawn us into vicious coping cycles
- Process issues of abuse and abandonment and the unhealthy paths we often take to get through these issues
- Discover freedom from false intimacy and hope for lasting change

DISCOVERING THE TRUTH – 40 MINUTES

LEADER: *"Discovering the Truth" continues the discussion from Session 3 about what we're thirsty for. Read any explanations and questions aloud or ask for volunteers. Keep things moving and be sure to leave time for "Embracing the Truth" questions and the "Connecting" group experience that follow. Review the group's progress using the Pulling the Plug Schematic.*

DO I WANT TO GET WELL?
WHAT AM I THIRSTY FOR?
HOW CAN I BREAK THE CYCLE?
HOW WILL I COUNTERATTACK?
WHAT ARE MY DEEPEST LONGINGS?

       Am I willing to embrace my pain?

       What will be my legacy?

CREATED FOR INTIMACY AND ECSTASY

It's no surprise that prostitution is one of the world's oldest professions and that the sales of pornography dwarfs all other industries on the Internet. We are sexual beings; God designed us that way from the beginning. As we discussed in Session 1, sex is a key target of the Enemy because it's an area in which we're vulnerable and because it so closely reflects the intimacy of God the Father, God the Son, and God the Holy Spirit.

4 Long before [God] laid down earth's foundations, he had us in mind, had settled on us as the focus of his love, to be made whole and holy by his love. 5 Long, long ago he decided to adopt us into his family through Jesus Christ. (What pleasure he took in planning this!) 6 He wanted us to enter into the celebration of his lavish gift-giving by the hand of his beloved Son. 7 Because of the sacrifice of the Messiah, his blood poured out on the altar of the Cross, we're a free people—free of penalties and punishments chalked up by all our misdeeds. And not just barely free, either. Abundantly free!

EPHESIANS 1:4-7, THE MESSAGE

As a bridegroom rejoices over his bride, so will your God rejoice over you. ISAIAH 62:5, NIV

2 When you're in over your head, I'll be there with you. When you're in rough waters, you will not go down. When you're between a rock and a hard place, it won't be a dead end—3Because I am GOD, your personal God, The Holy of Israel, your Savior. I paid a huge price for you: all of Egypt, with rich Cush and Seba thrown in! 4 That's how much you mean to me! That's how much I love you! I'd sell off the whole world to get you back, trade the creation just for you.

ISAIAH 43:2-4, THE MESSAGE

> LEADER: *Discuss as many discovery questions as time permits. There's extra information to read aloud on the desires of the heart and the walking wounded. Consider asking some members to share this task with you. It will help to highlight in advance the questions/information you don't want to miss.*

1. What does it mean to be the "focus" of someone's love (Ephesians 1:4)? How does a bridegroom feel about his new bride (Isaiah 62:5)?

2. How would a bride feel if her lover would give away everything in exchange for her love (Isaiah 43:4)?

3. What other phrases in Ephesians 1:4-7 and Isaiah 43:2-4 explain the depth of God's desire for a deep, personal relationship with you?

4. In what various ways is a strong husband-wife relationship more intimate and ecstasy-filled than any other human relationship? What does the lover-bride image tell us about the depth of intimacy and ecstasy for which God created us?

DESIRES OF THE HEART

Maybe breaking free from sex addictions would be easier if the problem simply boiled down to lust, but that's far too simplistic. Just as a healthy sexual relationship is a sign of a healthy marriage relationship, unhealthy sexual practices are a sign of more complex issues in our lives.

5. What would you say are some of the key needs and desires men generally seek to fulfill? Where do men typically search in an attempt to find satisfaction and fulfillment in life?

Many of us find it difficult to identify what we think, feel, want, and need. We're even likely to hear: "Why don't you get honest about your thoughts and feelings?" The problem is that too often we really don't have a clue about what we really feel or want.

Social science and clinical practice point to seven core desires that men share to which we are deeply connected.

Men desire to be respected and affirmed. All men want to be valued. The support and respect of others is tremendously important to a man's self-esteem. Mark Twain once said, "I can live for two months on a good compliment." Praise communicates your approval of an individual as a person.

Men desire to be included in an adventure. Each man wants to be a meaningful part of an important and noble adventure—something larger than himself.

Men desire to connect (touch in non-sexual ways). This is typically highlighted as a woman's desire, but regular physical contact through hugs, pats on the back, and the like is essential. Research at UCLA concluded that it takes 8-10 meaningful touches a day for a person to thrive. [1]

Men desire to be desired. Although men are taught to put on a tough exterior, if you're honest with yourself, you must admit that you long to be passionately wanted and needed by the woman in your life.

Men desire to be a hero. Men want demonstrate that they have what it takes to deliver, to come through, to protect, defend, and rescue. Men want to leave a legacy!

Men desire to feel be grounded and secure. Security includes physical needs like shelter, food, clothing, and enough money to feel comfortable. However, it extends far beyond that into emotional, relational, and spiritual stability.

Men desire to be heard. Few men have a friend or spouse will truly listen to what they have to say. A listening ear speaks volumes about our value to another person.

6. Which of these seven desires of the heart do you feel most fulfilled in at this point in your life? In which of these desires are you definitely unfulfilled?

WALKING WOUNDED

Ideally, all seven desires of the heart would be fulfilled as part of our childhood experiences. While nobody has perfect parents or a life without pain, some men grow up with few of these needs met well. Instead of being cared for, they were deeply wounded. When these desires go unmet, life becomes impaired. We may ultimately feel abandoned, isolated, and disillusioned.

We all experience pain in our lives at times and there are many ways for us to "numb out" or escape the pain. The Enemy strategically shoots arrows or uses the wounds in our lives to distort our identity—our perception of who we are. He then continually whispers lies about who we are, who God is, God's heart toward us, and the intimacy God wants us to share with Him. Ron Keck has developed the following model to describe the process of our hearts being captured and enslaved.

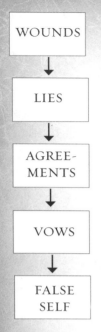

- Strategic ARROWS are launched into our lives to create WOUNDS: *A difficult loss ... Painful circumstances ... Traumatic event ... Neglect ... Abuse*

- Our WOUNDS become infected with LIES or false beliefs: *"God has abandoned me too" ... "I'm a failure" ... "Nobody cares; it's up to me to look out for me"*

- Satan repeats LIES until we make AGREEMENTS to accept them as truth: *"I'm on my own now" ... "There's no hope" ... I can't live without it" ... "This is all I deserve"*

- Once AGREEMENTS are made VOWS are soon to follow: *"I will never again ..." ... "From now on, I will always ..."*

- False agreements and vows feed the FALSE SELF: *Our distorted views about who we are ... The masks we wear to cover our true selves*

Jesus and Paul explained what goes on within our hearts:

[20] *[Jesus] added, "It is what comes from inside that defiles you. [21] For from within, out of a person's heart, come evil thoughts, sexual immorality, theft, murder, [22] adultery, greed, wickedness, deceit, lustful desires, envy, slander, pride, and foolishness. [23] All these vile things come from within; they are what defile you."*

Mark 7:20-23, NLT

[15] *For I do not understand what I am doing, because I do not practice what I want to do, but I do what I hate. [16] And if I do what I do not want to do, I agree with the law that it is good. [17] So now I am no longer the one doing it, but it is sin living in me.*

Romans 7:15-17, HCSB

7. According to Jesus in Mark 7:20-23, where do the lies, false agreements, and vows become embedded? What impact can these deeply rooted false beliefs have in our lives?

8. What's the inner struggle Paul is describing in Romans 7:15-17? What does Paul imply about his identity, the truest thing about himself? Whom or what does he conclude is doing these destructive things?

In his book *Out of the Shadows* (Hazeldon, 2001), Pat Carnes identifies the four core beliefs that abused and wounded children internalize. These false beliefs or lies pervade our culture in epidemic proportions because of deep wounds and unmet needs:

(1) I am a bad, unworthy person.

(2) No one will love me as I am.

(3) No one will take care of my needs but me.

(4) Sex is my most important need – Sex becomes deeply associated with the needs for love, nurture, and touch

EMBRACING THE TRUTH – 20 MINUTES

LEADER: This section focuses on helping group members integrate what they've learned from the Bible discussions into their own hearts and lives. As we seek healing, it's important to look to the wounds of our past and also to the intimacy counterfeits that we turn to in the present. As you open up and share from your own story, the other group members will feel more comfortable and safe.

THE THINGS WE WANT TO ESCAPE

Reliving the wounds of the past is painful, but if we want to heal then we must reopen our wounds and clean out the infections. Addictions often find their roots in either damaging *abuse* or *neglect* that occur early in life. The goal of understanding is not to blame, but rather to see the truth, to feel the hurt and anger, and then to constructively release the pain so healing can begin.

Depending on the severity of abuse and the individuals involved, a person may develop multiple addictive behaviors. For example, about 50% of sex addicts are alcoholics. In cases like this, recovery will be more complex, requiring more time and persistence.

ABUSE: Sins of commission, trauma events, or personal boundary violations

NEGLECT: Sins of omission, withholding something needed to thrive, or abandonment

1. As a group, list various examples of invasive abuse that children might experience? (Be sure to consider emotional, physical, sexual, and spiritual abuse.)

2. List various examples of harmful abandonment or neglect children might experience?

3. What was life like growing up in your home?

FALSE INTIMACY

In research of 1,000 sex addicts, Pat Carnes found 97% were emotionally abused, 74% physically abused, and 81% sexually abused (*Don't Call It Love*, Bantom, 1992). When we carry wounds of the past, we search desperately for something—anything—that will fill the empty places in our hearts. We become easy prey for counterfeits that promise to fulfill our desires. For example, masturbation, in addition to a hormonal experience, can be a way of self-gratification and self-medicating. On the surface, porno and other unhealthy sexual behaviors seem to address many desires. Let's see how God feels:

[*God speaking in metaphor:*] *"For My people have committed a double evil: They have abandoned Me, the fountain of living water, and dug cisterns for themselves, cracked cisterns that cannot hold water."*

JEREMIAH 2:13, HCSB

4. What do the cisterns in Jeremiah 2:13 represent? What happens when we fall into relying on our own resources rather than taking our deepest thirsts to God?

[21] *For although they knew God, they neither glorified him as God nor gave thanks to him, but their thinking became futile and their foolish hearts were darkened.* [22] *Although they claimed to be wise, they became fools* [23] *and exchanged the glory of the immortal God for images made to look like mortal man and birds and animals and reptiles.* [24] *Therefore God gave them over in the sinful desires of their hearts to sexual impurity for the degrading of their bodies with one another.* [25] *They exchanged the truth of God for a lie, and worshiped and served created things rather than the Creator—who is forever praised. ...* [28] *he gave them over to a depraved mind, to do what ought not to be done.* [29] *They have become filled with every kind of wickedness, evil, greed and depravity.*

ROMANS 1:21-25, 28-29, NIV

5. Why do you think that we so easily abandon God in exchange for counterfeit lovers—our addictions (Romans 1:21-23)?

6. How does God respond when we seek to fulfill our deepest longings with substitutes rather than wrestling with what prevents intimacy with Him (verses 24-29)? Why do you think we settle for substitutes?

The old adage is true: "We're lookin' for love in all the wrong places." We long for a deep connection, real intimacy, nurture, and affirmation. As we turn to the false substitutes, we find ourselves in a vicious cycle. We use unhealthy sexual behaviors to escape our pain, only to find ourselves empty, ashamed, and even more hurt. And then, to cope with the emptiness and the pain, we start the cycle all over again.

NOTE: Because of our fear of abandonment or need for affirmation, we are likely to project these desires onto our wives or girlfriends, expecting them to be the all-nurturing females that will meet our every need. The obsessive pattern of seeking another person's approval and validation rather than drawing this from within ourselves and from God is what therapists refer to as "codependency." Men who don't know how to engage in or express intimacy can substitute the act of sex for nurture and caring so it becomes a "false intimacy." Wives recognize intuitively what's happening and know that our attempts to be intimate aren't real, so resistance surfaces. On the other hand, the women in our fantasies and at the local club always say "yes" and seem to like everything about us.

CONNECTING – 15 MINUTES

LEADER: Use "Connecting" as a time to help group members deepen their connection with each other, with God, and with their own hearts. As always, be prepared to share your story first to set the tone of openness and trust. Remind everyone that this is a safe environment where you're standing together like the gladiators in the Coliseum.

All the false substitutes the world offers can never satisfy us the way genuine intimacy with God can. In order to find healing, men addicted to pornography and other sexual activities must begin to acknowledge that all of their strivings to satisfy their thirsts are extreme failures.

STANDING TOGETHER

Deep down we feel successful if our lives are neat and in order, and we feel like unlovable failures if our lives are messy. Facing what's inside ourselves and breaking the strangle hold of secrecy can be very difficult, but are vital to healing. The experience your group leader is about to share with you requires some level of openness with one another, but it will be very insightful to each person in the group and will strengthen you as a supportive, healing community.

LEADER INSTRUCTIONS FOR THE SUGGESTED GROUP EXPERIENCE:

(1) CIRCLE UP: Including yourself, divide the group in half (one half may have an extra person). Ask half the group to gather their seats in a circle and sit facing one another.

(2) EXPLAIN: Each person standing needs to think of a short response to the following two statements. Read both statements aloud, then repeat them:

"The root desire I believe I'm trying to fulfill with my secret seductress is _____ *,"* and
"The most difficult thing for me about dumping my secret seductress is _____*."*

(3) SET UP: Give a minute or so for the standing people to think about their responses. Meanwhile, explain to the seated people that they should close their eyes and place both hands with palms up on the table or their laps. This signifies carrying the burdens of the people who speak from their hearts. Ask the standing people to gather around the outside of the circle, with one person standing behind each seated person.

(4) EXPLAIN: Each person standing will lean down and share his responses in the right ear of the seated person. Then, each standing person will step to the right behind the next seated person and repeat those responses. Those standing will continue stepping to the right and speaking to each seated person until they're back where they started. REPEAT: Read the two statements again as review before the standing people begin.

(5) GO: When everyone has some kind of response (it does not have to be earth-shaking), instruct the standing group to begin. When the circuit is completed, ask the people sitting to share any thoughts or feelings about what they heard. This is always amazingly insightful!

(6) SWITCH: Ask the seated and standing people to switch positions. Repeat this exercise with the new standing group.

We discussed in Session 3 how secrets, shame, and shadows are tools of the Enemy to keep us in bondage to our addictions and sins. It can be frightening to open up and break the power of secrecy, but when we release our secrets to others who trust and care about us, it's a huge relief. In the same way, being truly open about our feelings with God will take us on the path to healing, but most of us have doubts about God's goodness and, specifically, about His heart toward us personally. Let's end our session by looking at God's desire for us as He discusses His eternal kingdom:

¹¹ On that day you will not be put to shame for all the wrongs you have done to me, because I will remove from this city those who rejoice in their pride. Never again will you be haughty on my holy hill. ¹² But I will leave within you the meek and humble, who trust in the name of the LORD. ... ¹⁵ The LORD has taken away your punishment, he has turned back your enemy. The LORD, the King of Israel, is with you; never again will you fear any harm. ... ¹⁷ The LORD your God is with you, he is mighty to save. He will take great delight in you, he will quiet you with his love, he will rejoice over you with singing."

ZEPHANIAH 3:11-12,15,17, NIV

1. God promises that He won't put His children to shame (verse 11) and will take away our punishment (verse 15). What vital heart attitudes does God identify in verses 11-12 that we must embrace to be saved?

2. What does verse 17 tell you about God's heart toward you personally? How does it make you feel when you hear that God takes "great delight in you" and "rejoices over you with singing"?

MY PRAYER NEEDS:

MY GROUP'S PRAYER NEEDS:

LEADER: *Close by praying for the various struggles that were shared in the circle experience. Be sure to remind everyone to spend time with the "Taking It Home" questions this week.*

TAKING IT HOME

While we need to continue to break free and stay free with accountability measures, the focus in this session on healing from the inside out must be our long-term goal. Take the following questions to your heart and to God as another step on the journey.

QUESTIONS TO TAKE TO MY HEART

The following questions ask you to look into your heart and consider with brutal honesty your deepest feelings and beliefs. Consider everything you've learned in this study so far. Remember, our behaviors are the best indicator of what we truly believe in our innermost being (Psalm 51:6). Be sure to journal your thoughts, struggles, and insights.

Look back over the seven desires of the heart listed in the "Discovering the Truth" section from this session. Spend some time of introspection and ask yourself:

✳ What's behind my fascination with porn? Why is it that I really prefer porn or other counterfeit lovers to intimacy with God? With my wife?

✳ What do I really believe about God and intimacy with Him?

Journal Exercise

Use the journal space on page 91 to jot down times when your secret seductress calls to you or tempts you. Each time this occurs, stop and strive to understand what's going on in your innermost being. What needs or desires of the heart are crying out? What lies do you still believe? What false agreements and vows are you making about yourself, God, your secret seductress, or other people? Review the list often, and continue to add to it, paying attention to deeper desires and longings that surface.

1 "Helping engaged couples find A.W.E. in their upcoming marriage," Jim Burns, Pastors.com [cited 19 January 2007]. Available on the Internet: http://www.pastors.com/article.asp?ArtID=9716.

DESIRES OF THE HEART JOURNAL

AM I WILLING TO EMBRACE MY PAIN?

BREAKING THE ICE – 10 MINUTES

LEADER: By now your group should be connecting well and supporting each other toward recovery. Even though the group is now used to deeper discussions, start out with some lighthearted "Breaking the Ice" questions. Choose only one of the first two questions. (Alternative: Ask the guys in your group to do impersonations if some of them are good at this.) Be sure to discuss questions 3 and 4.

OPTIONAL MOVIE NIGHT: Since the movie The Legend of Bagger Vance *plays such a central role in Session 7, we would encourage you to set up an additional meeting to watch the film together and be prepared to discuss it. The one sexual situation is a good illustration of false intimacy.*

1. Which of the following substitutes do you find most annoying? Why?

   ❑ Artificial sweeteners ❑ Imitation wood grain
   ❑ Cosmetic surgery, wigs, toupees ❑ Imitation leather or fake fur
   ❑ Imitation crabmeat ❑ Fake friendliness
   ❑ Athletes on steroids ❑ Dyed or sprayed-on hair
   ❑ Phonies playing big man—putting on airs
   ❑ Other: _____

2. I wish I could imitate ...

   ❑ Tiger Wood's golf swing
   ❑ Warren Buffet's ability to pick stocks
   ❑ _____'s ability as a musician' or artist
   ❑ LeBron James' dunk
   ❑ Lance Armstrong's courage, determination, and muscle tone
   ❑ _____'s gift as a writer
   ❑ Bill Cosby's parenting style
   ❑ _____'s effectiveness as a speaker
   ❑ Other: _____

3. The best trade I ever made or the best deal I ever negotiated was: _____
_____. What did it take to pull this off?

4. As you spent time this week examining your heart and listening to God, what insights did you gain into the deep desires of your heart or your true beliefs about God and intimacy with him?

OPENING PRAYER

God, we're actually pretty good at doing impersonations. We've learned to play the role of the "nice Christian man" or the "faithful Christian husband." We're not really faking those identities—we usually are those men, just not all the time. Most of the people closest to us don't have a clue. But we know. You know. And our band of brothers knows. Lord, we're tired of living a double life. We want to be faithful and pure, but left to ourselves we do a poor imitation of You. Don't leave us alone ... even when we try to hide. Come find us. Hold us close. Heal us. Set us free!

OBJECTIVES FOR THIS SESSION

• Review the process of shame and addiction

• Understand the process of change, healing, and wholeness

• Learn to address the wounds of the past by embracing our pain and rejecting our shame

• Begin eliminating distorted views of God and deepening our trust in Him to lead us to a life that's wildly free

DISCOVERING THE TRUTH — 30 MINUTES

LEADER: *"Discovering the Truth" focuses on finding the motivation and understanding the process to break free from the cycle of shame and addiction. Read any explanations and questions aloud or ask for volunteers. Be sure to leave ample time for the questions and group experiences in the "Embracing the Truth" and "Connecting" segments. Using the Pulling the Plug Schematic, highlight the significant strides each person in the group has made, while acknowledging that the brutal battle for freedom and life is has only begun.*

In the last session, we acknowledged the vicious coping cycle we get trapped in as we seek to fulfill legitimate needs and desires through fakes or counterfeits ... as we try to escape or numb the pain in our lives, or ... as we act on lies we've accepted as truth. To break out of this cycle for good, we need supernatural power and intense motivation.

DO I WANT TO GET WELL?
WHAT AM I THIRSTY FOR?
HOW CAN I BREAK THE CYCLE?
HOW WILL I COUNTERATTACK?
WHAT ARE MY DEEPEST LONGINGS?
AM I WILLING TO EMBRACE MY PAIN?
What will be my legacy?

Compelling Motivation: Gaining Something More Valuable

As we stop the rendezvous with our secret seductresses, we've won a battle but not the war. They relentlessly coax us back. These deceiving lovers draw us back into slavery by promising ecstasy but delivering emptiness, shame, and despair. Sacrifices, risks, and deep soul changes will not happen unless we have a compelling reason. The pain that brought us into this group can be a strong motivator, but so can the promise of great reward.

44 The kingdom of heaven is like treasure, buried in a field, that a man found and reburied. Then in his joy he goes and sells everything he has and buys that field. 45 Again, the kingdom of heaven is like a merchant in search of fine pearls. 46 When he found one priceless pearl, he went and sold everything he had, and bought it.

MATTHEW 13:44-46, HCSB

LEADER: Discuss as many discovery questions as time permits. Help group members to grasp what they've been trading off. Read the questions and explanations aloud. It will help to highlight in advance the questions you don't want to miss.

1. What do Jesus' two analogies in Matthew 13:44-46 show us about the kingdom of heaven? Why do you think the kingdom of heaven is more valuable than anything?

[1] *[Jesus speaking to His followers:]* *"Don't let your hearts be troubled. Trust in God, and trust also in me.* [2] *There is more than enough room in my Father's home. If this were not so, would I have told you that I am going to prepare a place for you?* [3] *When everything is ready, I will come and get you, so that you will always be with me where I am.*

JOHN 14:1-3, NLT

In Luke 17:21 Jesus says, "The kingdom of God is among you," clarifying that the priceless value of the kingdom is in a person, not a place. A deep relationship with Jesus is worth huge sacrifices, bringing great value in this life and value beyond imagination in eternity.

2. Jesus has gone away as a bridegroom does to prepare a new home for His bride. What is Jesus anxiously anticipating in the kingdom of heaven (John 14:3)? How do the things we gain from our secret seductresses compare to Jesus' offer of eternal ecstasy?

OLD RUTS

The path to healing and wholeness, freedom and life, requires commitment to a long journey filled with ups and downs. It's difficult to leave well-worn paths—those familiar patterns of thought and behavior that we've depended on to cope and survive since we were children. Our old habit patterns and ways of coping are killing our hearts, our relationships, and our souls, yet they feel like a vital part of who we are.

The Bible warns us that disconnecting from counterfeit lovers and reconnecting deeply with God is always a struggle:

[18] *With an appeal to twisted sexual desires, they lure back into sin those who have barely escaped from a lifestyle of deception.* [19] *They promise freedom, but they themselves are slaves of sin and corruption. For you are a slave to whatever controls you.* [20] *And when people escape from the wickedness of the world by knowing our Lord and Savior Jesus Christ and then get tangled up and enslaved by sin again, they are worse off than before. ...* [22] *They prove the truth of this proverb: "A dog returns to its vomit." And another says, "A washed pig returns to the mud."*

2 PETER 2:18B-20,22, NLT

3. According to verse 18, what two distortions in our hearts and minds got us into trouble in the first place and set us up to be pulled back in?

4. What would have to happen to a dog in order to keep it from returning to its vomit or to a pig to keep it from wallowing in the mud? What can we learn from these examples about finding real change and freedom in our own lives?

In *The Weight of Glory,* C. S. Lewis explains how we are both drawn to relational intimacy and, at the same time, fear and avoid it: "We are half-hearted creatures, fooling about with drink and sex and ambition [or anything else we give our lives to] when infinite joy is offered us, like an ignorant child who wants to go on making mud pies in a slum because he cannot imagine what is meant by an offer of a holiday at the sea. We are far too easily pleased." [1]

PROCESS OF HEALING

We've learned that to experience healing, we must address the fantasy (secrets), despair (shadows), and shame that lie beneath the behaviors. Fantasy is not the primary problem, it's a symptom of our emotional and spiritual condition. Fantasies accomplish three objectives: (1) distracting us from painful emotions, (2) meeting otherwise unmet desires and needs, and (3) recasting our experiences of past abuse.

5. To which objectives of fantasy can you relate? What ways have you tried or been told about to stop sexual fantasies? How effective have these approaches been?

6. What strategies have you tried to eliminate shadows, phantoms, and shame in your life? How effective have these approaches been?

Traditional approaches for stopping fantasies are ineffective because they don't address the root issues. Rather than ignoring our fantasies, we need to understand that they are symptoms. We need to identify and uncover the wounds of abuse or neglect they reveal. Rather than resigning to live without hope, we can allow despair to force us to accept our need for God, who longs to give us a new vision for ourselves and our lives. To deal with unhealthy shame, we must delve into the trauma and wounds in our past, allowing God to replace our shame with grace and true intimacy.

The following charts clearly demonstrate that sexual addiction is powerful because it attempts to manage the unhealthy sense of shame that stems from past trauma and wounds. The healing journey must address and reverse each step on the journey that leads to sexual addiction.

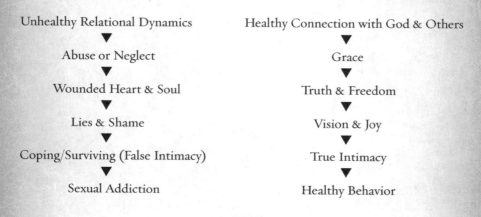

JOURNEY OF SHAME & ADDICTION	JOURNEY OF HEALING
Unhealthy Relational Dynamics	Healthy Connection with God & Others
▼	▼
Abuse or Neglect	Grace
▼	▼
Wounded Heart & Soul	Truth & Freedom
▼	▼
Lies & Shame	Vision & Joy
▼	▼
Coping/Surviving (False Intimacy)	True Intimacy
▼	▼
Sexual Addiction	Healthy Behavior

Embracing the Truth – 35 minutes

LEADER: This section focuses on helping group members take the next steps in the healing journey of replacing their distorted beliefs and behavioral ruts with truth and healthy behaviors. As we seek healing, it's important to identify and process the wounds from our past and break the barriers these have erected to health and wholeness. Continue to open up and share your own story to encourage group members in their struggles.

Long and Winding Road

The journey into sexual addiction takes decades, likely beginning in childhood. Recall from Session 6 that 70-80% of sex addicts have experienced some form of physical and/or sexual abuse, and nearly all have experienced emotional abuse or neglect. Whether abuse or abandonment, the wounds are deep, requiring years of recovery. The first two years are the most intense period of healing, but as we commit to the journey, God will lead us into increasingly more freedom, healing, and intimacy.

Referring to "idols"—those things we give our lives to, turn to in times of need, and bow down to or worship—God explains how the failures and woundedness of people can do incredible damage in the hearts and lives of their children:

You must not bow down to them or worship them, for I, the LORD *your God, am a jealous God who will not tolerate your affection for any other gods. I lay the sins of the parents upon their children; the entire family is affected—even children in the third and fourth generations of those who reject me.*

EXODUS 20:5, NLT

1. In what ways does God sound like a deeply-committed husband and lover of His people?

2. Discuss examples from your own lives of sins, failures, or wounds that have been passed down to you from your parents or their parents.

BACK INTO THE SHADOWS

LEADER INSTRUCTIONS FOR THE GROUP EXPERIENCE: Have a TV/DVD player set up. Read the following introduction to the group, and then show a scene from the 2000 film, The Legend of Bagger Vance, *starring Will Smith, Matt Damon, and Charlize Theron. Show part of Chapter 29 "The Drop" (begin about 4 minutes in at 1:37:08 and continue to end of Chapter 29 at 1:43:35 on the DVD timer). After showing the clip, discuss the following questions.*

The Legend of Bagger Vance *is used as the basis for the rest of this session. Either pick key areas to discuss and keep things moving, or propose expanding this to cover two meetings.*

Director Robert Redford explains that the film is "about a man who's lost his authentic swing." He describes the journey of a man "who falls into darkness through some disconnect with his soul, and then of his coming back into the light with the help of a spiritual guide." In Junuh's story, the disconnect happened during traumatic events in combat when men under his leadership were slaughtered. Finding his authentic golf swing is symbolic of rediscovering and redeeming his life.

3. Alone in the woods, the full force of Junuh's trauma came flooding back. What do you think was going through his mind? Discuss the various intense feelings he displayed.

4. When he entered the woods, Junuh's focus was on the darkness that surrounded him rather than on the light—the way out. He was ready to give up in despair and shame. According to Lamentations 3:17-20, what are some lies that become deeply embedded into the wounds in our hearts and can lead us to despair?

[Jeremiah shares his true feelings in a difficult time:] ¹⁷ I gave up on life altogether. I've forgotten what the good life is like. ¹⁸ I said to myself, "This is it. I'm finished. God is a lost cause." ¹⁹ I'll never forget the trouble, the utter lostness, the taste of ashes, the poison I've swallowed. ²⁰ I remember it all—oh, how well I remember—the feeling of hitting the bottom.

LAMENTATIONS 3:17-20, THE MESSAGE

5. What key truth did Bagger reveal to Junuh about his burden and what he needed to do with it? How does this correspond to Jesus' promise in Matthew 5:4, and why is remembering and grieving our losses so vital in healing from hurts and traumas?

Blessed are those who mourn, because they will be comforted.   MATTHEW 5:4, HCSB

6. What critical formula for healing (that we often get backwards) does Jesus model for us in Hebrews 12:2?

... keeping our eyes on Jesus, the source and perfecter of our faith, who for the joy that lay before Him endured a cross and despised the shame, and has sat down at the right hand of God's throne.

HEBREWS 12:2, HCSB (EMPHASIS ADDED)

Bagger says, "Ain't a soul on this earth ain't got a burden to carry he don't understand." Like many of us, Junuh allowed his wounds, his failures, his burden, to define him. We try to escape rather than remembering our wounds and staying in our pain until we figure out the path to "find our swing." Unwilling to face our intense emotions or to take responsibility about where we go from here, we let our burdens become our identity, we accept lies about ourselves and God, and we settle for survival in place of real life.

The battle Junuh waged in the shadows is the same one we each fight—the battle for our hearts and the legacy of our lives.

³ For though we live in the world, we do not wage war as the world does. ⁴ The weapons we fight with are not the weapons of the world. On the contrary, they have <u>divine power to demolish strongholds.</u> ⁵ We demolish arguments and every pretension that sets itself up against the knowledge of God, and we take captive every thought to make it obedient to Christ.

2 CORINTHIANS 10:3-5, NIV

7. In 2 Corinthians 10:4-5, Paul talks about demolishing "strongholds." When you imagine castles and fortified strongholds, what does it take to demolish them? Using this illustration, what kind of battle and reconstruction process would you envision to demolish the lies and deceiving voices that hold us captive?

Just as when Bagger said the memories Junuh was trying to recall were "just a moment ago," our deepest hurts are just below the surface even if inflicted long ago. The first step to healing is recognizing the abuse for what it was. It typically takes time, even years, to identify and process all our wounds, but it begins as we "stand real still and remember."

When Junuh struggled to remember his pain and his authentic swing, Bagger gave incredible assurance in the same way God speaks to us: "You ain't alone. I'm right here with you. I've been here all along."

¹ Do not be afraid, for I have ransomed you. I have called you by name; you are mine. ² When you go through deep waters, I will be with you. When you go through rivers of difficulty, you will not drown. When you walk through the fire of oppression, you will not be burned up; the flames will not consume you. ³ For I am the LORD, your God, the Holy One of Israel, your Savior.

ISAIAH 43:1B-3A, NLT

Fear is often the greatest enemy to meaningful life change. We long to return to what's familiar rather than take risks and face the fear of the unknown.

8. What assurances does God give in Isaiah 43:1-3 for the various fears we might face? Which of these assurances gives you the greatest comfort? Explain.

CONNECTING — 15 MINUTES

LOOSEN YOUR GRIP

Part of Bagger's counsel to Junuh was to loosen his grip and to settle himself. If we're going to take advantage of the divinely powerful weapons we need for healing, we'll have to loosen our grip on our wounds and our coping mechanisms. God is a gentleman and will not force Himself into our lives; He waits to be invited in and continually extends an invitation to us.

[Jesus invites us:] ²⁸ *"Are you tired? Worn out? Burned out on religion? Come to me. Get away with me and you'll recover your life. I'll show you how to take a real rest.* ²⁹ *Walk with me and work with me—watch how I do it. Learn the unforced rhythms of grace. I won't lay anything heavy or ill-fitting on you.* ³⁰ *Keep company with me and you'll learn to live freely and lightly."*

MATTHEW 11:28-30, THE MESSAGE

1. What does Jesus say we need to do to find real rest and recover our lives? What would you have to change in your heart and mind to enable you to embrace rest and accept Jesus' offer to walk with Him, work with Him, and learn the unforced rhythms of grace?

COMING OUT OF THE SHADOWS

After Junuh let himself remember his trauma, recall a time when he had his authentic swing, and loosen his grip to trust Bagger, it was time to launch out of the shadows and into the light. Bagger told him, "It's time for you to come on out of the shadows ... strike that ball Junuh. Don't hold nothin' back; give it everything! ... let it be your swing. Now is the time!" God urges each of us in this same way.

[God says:] I will say to the prisoners, "Come out in freedom," and to those in darkness, "Come into the light." They will be my sheep, grazing in green pastures and on hills that were previously bare.

ISAIAH 49:9, NLT

[God speaking:] I will lead the blind by ways they have not known, along unfamiliar paths I will guide them; I will turn the darkness into light before them and make the rough places smooth. These are the things I will do; I will not forsake them.

ISAIAH 42:16, NIV

2. According to Isaiah 49:9, what is God's desire for you? What would it look like for you right now to hold nothing back—to fight for freedom and healing with everything you've got?

3. In what ways do you feel "blind" as you take this recovery path? What's your deepest concern or fear about taking the unfamiliar path to healing (Isaiah 42:16)?

4. What's the worst thing that could happen as you loosen your grip and allow God to take you back into your pain and shadows? What could this group do to help you risk the next step you know you need to take?

More than anything else, the healing journey requires us to trust God. Healing the wounds in our innermost being will lead us down paths we never could have imagined. We must take one day and one step at a time as we walk into the shadows with Jesus, allow Him to turn the shadows to light, ease our pain, and lead us into freedom, truth, and the true desires of our hearts.

Each victory builds confidence, but victories can also bring overconfidence. Failing to follow the path God lays out for us can lead to defeat and discouragement. We will continue to question God and be tempted to turn away from Him to go our own way. The healing journey brings a constant challenge to trust God more.

My Prayer Requests & Support Needs:

My Group's Prayer Requests & Support Needs:

LEADER: Close by praying for each individual that he would journey back into the shadows of his life with Jesus at his side, learning to trust Jesus more and more as He leads him on the unfamiliar paths to freedom, healing, and life. Remind everyone to spend time with the "Taking It Home" questions this week.

TAKING IT HOME

While we need to continue to break free and stay free with accountability measures, the focus in this session on healing from the inside out must be our long-term goal. Take the following questions to your heart and to God as another step on the journey.

QUESTIONS TO TAKE TO MY HEART

Ask your heart the following questions to identify deep-rooted lies that could stem from abuse or abandonment issues. Remember, it's our behaviors rather than our intellectual declarations that are the best indicators of what we truly believe in our innermost being (Psalm 51:6). Consider what your behaviors tell you about what you really believe. Be sure to journal your thoughts, struggles, and insights.

✳ In which of the following beliefs do I clearly struggle? What is driving each of these destructive beliefs? Why do I struggle with these specific issues? (NOTE: keep asking "why?" until you discover some root causes or events.)

❏ I am a bad, unworthy person; nobody likes me.

❏ God has abandoned me too.

❏ No one will love me as I am. Nobody would like me if they really knew me.

❏ I'm all alone, so it's up to me to take care of me.

❏ Sex is my most important need; it can meet my deepest needs and desires.

❏ Sex (or my porn addiction) is critical to my survival; I won't be able to cope without it.

❏ I'm a failure anyway so why even try?

❏ I live with shame all the time. My addictions and acting out are the truest things about me.

❏ I loathe myself for who I am and what I do.

❏ I must find a way to avoid the pain and isolation.

❏ There's no hope.

❏ This is all I deserve.

❏ Other: _____

QUESTIONS TO TAKE TO GOD

When you ask God a question, expect His Spirit to respond to your heart and spirit. Be careful not to rush it or manufacture an answer. Don't write down what you think is the "right answer." Don't turn the Bible into a reference book or spiritual encyclopedia. Just pose your question to God and wait on Him to answer. The litmus test for anything we hear from God is alignment with the Bible as our ultimate source of truth. Focus on listening to God, and record what you hear and sense He is saying to you.

✳ God, what do You want to say to me about my wounds/burdens?

✳ What do You want to say to me about joining You on the unfamiliar path?

Journal Exercise

Use the journal space on page 106 to begin to identify and capture various wounds and burdens you've been carrying. With each wound or burden identified, try to process the corresponding lie you've accepted and some events that sliced open and infected the wounds. Review the list often, adding to it as you regularly just stand still and remember.

Example: "I'm afraid that other people and even God will abandon me. I remember the pain when my stepfather said things like, 'You're as useless as ...' and 'I wish I had a son, a real son of my own.'"

1 C.S. Lewis, *The Weight of Glory* (San Francisco: Harper, 2001.)

Wounds and Memories Journal

WHAT WILL BE MY LEGACY?

BREAKING THE ICE – 10 MINUTES

> *LEADER: Because this is the final session of* The Secret Seductress, *you may want to allow even more personal sharing than in previous sessions. Group members now have the map for the journey to healing, but the journey has really only begun. Be sensitive to the group's need for closure as well as continued support as this study is wrapping up.*

1. What would your friends or family say that you are "famous" for?

2. Describe the biggest mess you've ever had to clean up.

3. What did you discover as you spent time this week considering the lies that might be embedded in your heart? Which false belief plagues you the most? What do you think is behind this belief?

4. What did you hear from God about trusting Him to heal you and redeem your life?

OPENING PRAYER

Jesus, we're just beginning to learn to rest in You, in the unforced rhythms of grace. We still struggle to understand the depth of Your feelings for us, but we're thankful. We long for a life filled with rich relationships, adventure, and meaning. As we continue to walk unfamiliar paths with You, we beg You to bring light to the dark recesses of our souls. We ask that you come against the Enemy who continues to be ruthless and cunning in his goal to destroy us, our relationships, and our legacies. Keep Your vision for our lives ever before us. Help us to learn to grow through our pain, and reject the shame the Enemy continually hurls at us. Be our Rescuer and Redeemer.

OBJECTIVES FOR THIS SESSION

- Summarize the steps to healing wounds of abuse and abandonment
- Choose a life of rich relationships, adventure, and meaning
- Engage the second compelling reason to stay in the battle to recapture our lives
- Decide what kind of legacy we want to leave and ignite a new vision
- Begin the journey toward healthy ways of relating to God and others
- Identify key truths and resources for continuing the journey

DISCOVERING THE TRUTH – 35 MINUTES

LEADER: *"Discovering the Truth" begins by summarizing the steps for healing our wounds. The bulk of the discussion centers around the legacy we'll leave. Read any explanations and questions aloud or ask for volunteers. Be sure to leave ample time for "Embracing the Truth" questions and the "Connecting" wrap-up. Use the Pulling the Plug Schematic to highlight the significant strides each person in the group has made, while acknowledging the ongoing battle for healing and wholeness has only begun.*

DO I WANT TO GET WELL?
WHAT AM I THIRSTY FOR?
HOW CAN I BREAK THE CYCLE?
HOW WILL I COUNTERATTACK?
WHAT ARE MY DEEPEST LONGINGS?
AM I WILLING TO EMBRACE MY PAIN?
WHAT WILL BE MY LEGACY?

Ain't Done Yet ...

In Session 7, we focused on healing the wounds of abuse and abandonment. We delved into the some of the steps, but in summary the progression of steps is:

• Understand the abuse and accept what happened to you.

• Accept the abuse and express your anger in healthy ways.

• Embrace the process of grieving the losses in your life.

• Confront your abuser (indirect confrontation through role-play or writing letters that will never be sent is typically very effective and less damaging to future reconciliation).

• Take the journey toward forgiving your abuser.

• Find meaning in your pain as a way to spiritual transformation, to deepen your relationship with Jesus and others, and to connect to the pain of others.

1. Where do you see yourself on the journey to healing your wounds? What is your greatest need in this process?

In the scene from *The Legend of Bagger Vance*, Junuh emerges from the woods after winning a huge spiritual victory—an incredible ending to a hard fought battle. But the story doesn't end there. Bagger's final comment wisely depicts the status of Junuh's journey: "Ain't done yet." If we remove the destructive patterns from our lives we win a huge victory, but we can't stop there. Jesus explains the spiritual dynamic with an example:

23 "Anyone who isn't with me opposes me, and anyone who isn't working with me is actually working against me. 24 When an evil spirit leaves a person, it goes into the desert, searching for rest. But when it finds none, it says, 'I will return to the person I came from.' 25 So it returns and finds that its former home is all swept and in order. 26 Then the spirit finds seven other spirits more evil than itself, and they all enter the person and live there. And so that person is worse off than before."

LUKE 11:23-26, NLT

LEADER: *Discuss as many discovery questions as time permits. Help group members to see the power of developing a God-given vision. If you like, you may opt to show the scene in the woods again from* The Legend of Bagger Vance. *Read the questions and explanations aloud. It will help to highlight in advance the questions you don't want to miss.*

2. The truths in Jesus' story of the evil spirits also apply to addictions and other destructive patterns in our lives. According to verses 25-26, what happens when we sweep the messes from our "houses," but then leave them vacant? What can we put into our souls to fill the void that's left when we remove the trash?

VISION

While we do need to place boundaries of protection around our lives, creating a godly vision for our lives is more powerful in helping us to live pure lives than avoidance alone. Just as fantasies are the starting point for sexual acting out, visions are the starting point for an awakening of the heart and to healthy ways of relating to God and others.

Fantasies are mental pictures of our own attempts to heal our wounds. Visions are mental pictures of God's grace and calling in our lives. This is the message of Jeremiah 2:13 about digging our own cisterns rather than turning to God with our passion and desires. In his book *What Jesus Demands from the World*, John Piper expresses it this way: "The root of sinfulness is the desire for our own happiness apart from God and apart from the happiness of others in God. ... All sin comes from a desire to be happy cut off from the glory of God and cut off from the good of others." [1]

[God speaking:] [11] I know what I'm doing. I have it all planned out—plans to take care of you, not abandon you, plans to give you the future you hope for. [12] When you call on me, when you come and pray to me, I'll listen. [13] When you come looking for me, you'll find me. Yes, when you get serious about finding me and want it more than anything else, [14] I'll make sure you won't be disappointed.

JEREMIAH 29:11-14A, THE MESSAGE

[Jesus speaking:] Seek the Kingdom of God above all else, and live righteously, and he will give you everything you need.

MATTHEW 6:33, NLT

3. According to Jeremiah 29:11-14 and Matthew 6:33, what benefits do we receive if we take on God's vision for our lives? How does that correspond with our desire to be involved in an adventure and our desire to be a hero?

During the scene in the woods, Bagger Vance helps Junuh see a picture of his role in the larger story when he urges, "Play the game—your game—the one that only you were meant to play; the one that was given to you when you came into this world. ... Now is the time, Junuh. Let it be your swing ..."

4. Do you know the vision God has for you? Have you discovered the role that only you were meant to play? How do you think pursuing that vision with everything you have will affect your life?

COMPELLING MOTIVATION: LEAVING SOMETHING VALUABLE

The first compelling motivation to persevere in a battle that requires sacrifices, risks, and deep soul changes is the promise of great reward. The second great motivator is the impact of what we will leave behind. We all want our lives to count for something— something that really will make a difference! God gives us a choice.

⁵... I, the LORD your God, am a jealous God who will not tolerate your affection for any other gods. I lay the sins of the parents upon their children; the entire family is affected—even children in the third and fourth generations of those who reject me. ⁶ But I lavish unfailing love for a thousand generations on those who love me and obey my commands.

EXODUS 20:5-6, NLT

THE LIES OF THE EYES

We can choose to live in selfishness or for the glory of God and the good of others.
    Sexual sin = normal sexual desire + selfishness
    Sexual purity = normal sexual desire + selflessness

Note that both sexual purity and sexual sin begin with normal sexual desire. The difference is the orientation of self. Sexual purity exercises selflessness and self-control while sexual sin indulges. "The Lies of the Eyes" shows the end result of the selfish road.

LEADER INSTRUCTIONS FOR THE GROUP EXPERIENCE: Page 4 shows a companion music CD called Somebody's Daughter *available from Serendipity House. Have a CD player queued up to play the poem "The Lies of the Eyes" from that CD. If you like, you can download lyrics from www.SerendipityHouse.com/Community (under Group Leaders - Leadership Aids). As group members listen, ask them to write down any thoughts or lines that affect them emotionally.*

5. What lines or thoughts from "The Lies of the Eyes" grabbed you? What were some lies of pornography that pulled the speaker into a life of destruction?

6. The man says, "The death I chose was deceptively slow. ... A corpse of a man, dead by indulgence at his own hand." What losses did the man experience as a result of his choices? What legacy did he leave behind? How is his legacy different than the legacy God offers us?

The poem concludes, "When a lie is a life, two choices remain: You can die in your strife or renounce it by name." We *will* all leave some kind of legacy. It all comes down to choosing what that legacy will be with our families, friends, and service to God.

7. Imagine your own funeral service. Your wife has the composure to make some remarks. One or more of your children want to speak. Other family and friends will share. Finally, God will sum up the substance and legacy of your life.

   • What do I want my wife to be able to say? Write it here.

   • What do I want my child(ren) to be able to say? Write it here.

   • What do I want other family and friends to be able to say? Write it here.

   • What would God say if my life continues down the path of sexual addiction? What do I want to hear Him say? Write it here.

> LEADER: *This section focuses on helping group members integrate various truths they've learned into their own hearts and lives. Encourage group members for any and all gains they've made through your time together studying* The Secret Seductress.

LOOKIN' FOR LOVE IN ALL THE RIGHT PLACES

As part of our ongoing healing journey, we must begin to develop healthy ways of relating to God and people. In the same way the evil spirits returned to ravage the vacancy left in the person's life (Luke 11:24-26), once we're free from a sexual addiction we still have a long way to go before we reach the finish line of real intimacy. Many sex addicts have lived for so long in false intimacy that they have no idea what real intimacy is.

1. How would you define emotional intimacy? Relational intimacy? Sexual intimacy? Spiritual Intimacy?

¹ Therefore if there is any encouragement in Christ, if there is any consolation of love, if there is any fellowship of the Spirit, if any affection and compassion, ² make my joy complete by being of the same mind, maintaining the same love, united in spirit, intent on one purpose. ³ Do nothing from selfishness or empty conceit, but with humility of mind regard one another as more important than yourselves; ⁴ do not merely look out for your own personal interests, but also for the interests of others.

PHILIPPIANS 2:1-4, NASB

¹² This is My command: love one another as I have loved you. ¹³ No one has greater love than this, that someone would lay down his life for his friends.

JOHN 15:12-13, HCSB

2. What aspects of healthy relationships are highlighted in Philippians 2:1-4? Are there others you would add?

3. Jesus laid His life down for us in every way possible. What are some ways in the normal course of life that a person can "lay down his life" for friends and family members (John 15:13)?

Relish life with the spouse you love each and every day of your precarious life. Each day is God's gift. It's all you get in exchange for the hard work of staying alive. Make the most of each one!

ECCLESIASTES 9:9, THE MESSAGE

⁶ Place me like a seal over your heart, like a seal on your arm. For love is as strong as death, its jealousy as enduring as the grave. Love flashes like fire, the brightest kind of flame. ⁷ Many waters cannot quench love, nor can rivers drown it. If a man tried to buy love with all his wealth, his offer would be utterly scorned.

SONG OF SONGS 8:6-7, NLT

4. According to Ecclesiastes 9:9, how should we approach intimacy in marriage?

5. The Song says, "Love is as strong as death." Describe what you think intimacy in marriage would look like if you could experience all the dimensions of love with this level of passion.

The opposite of sexual addiction is not abstinence. The opposite is deep relational connection, shared life, romance, respect, selflessness, and the joy of passionate intimacy based in a commitment that's as strong as death. Real intimacy takes time and effort to develop. God longs for this kind of intimacy with you, too.

² The nations will see your righteousness, and all kings your glory; and you will be called by a new name which the mouth of the LORD will designate. ³ You will also be a crown of beauty in the hand of the LORD, and a royal diadem in the hand of your God. ⁴ It will no longer be said to you, "Forsaken," nor to your land will it any longer be said, "Desolate;" but you will be called, "My delight is in her," and your land, "Married;" for the LORD delights in you, and to Him your land will be married. ⁵ For as a young man marries a virgin, so your sons will marry you; and as the bridegroom rejoices over the bride, so your God will rejoice over you.

ISAIAH 62:2-5, NASB

6. It's awkward for men to think in terms of being God's bride, but the relationship of lover to beloved is the deepest in our human experience. What words or phrases does God use in Isaiah 62:2-5 to describe the depth of His passion and commitment for you?

Intimacy does not magically replace the false intimacy that we've resigned ourselves to in the past. There are many forces in this world and in our hearts that fight against true intimacy. The choice is yours. Will you die in your strife or renounce it and cling to God with all that you have and all that you are?

CONNECTING — 20 MINUTES

LEADER: Use this final "Connecting" to launch group members as they continue on the healing journey. Review and discuss each of the key truths to remember. Make yourself and other group leaders available for ongoing support. Look for ways the group members can continue to support one another. Be sure to celebrate each man's progress!

STILL AIN'T DONE ...

Here are key truths to remember as you continue the healing journey:

• *WE'RE ONLY DUST.* God created us from dust and fully understands our human limitations and flaws.

• *DISTORTED DESIRES.* The goal is not to kill desire. Our needs and desires are not evil, but the ways we try to meet them are distorted. The problem too is that some desires have become distorted and need to be recalibrated by God.

• *EMBEDDED LIES.* The wounds in our lives and in our hearts have become infected with lies about God, ourselves, and the world in which we live.

• *GOD'S HEALING.* Everyone is broken, and God uses the difficult times in life to bring about our healing and redemption.

- *INTIMACY WITH GOD.* Pain and suffering are a path to knowing God with greater depth and authenticity.

- *STAYING IN THE PAIN.* Our natural tendency is to do anything but stay in our pain. But walking with God into the dark places of our hearts is vital for healing to occur.

- *LIFE'S MESSY.* Set your sights high, but don't be discouraged by bumps in the road.

- *VISION FOR LIFE.* Recovery and freedom is as much or more about what you do than what you don't do.

- *GOD'S PASSION.* God is contending passionately for you, and you never know what He is doing in the unseen realm. God is crazy about you and wants you to get well!

- *REJECT THE SHAME.* God's goal is not to condemn and shame you, but to rescue you, care for you, and redeem your life.

- *TAKE A JOURNEY.* We need a journey mentality rather than a destination mentality. Bagger Vance says, "It's a game that can't be won, only played." Stay committed to the journey. Healing, freedom, and eternal ecstasy await.

ONGOING SUPPORT SYSTEMS AS YOU CONTINUE THE JOURNEY,

MAKE ACCOUNTABILITY SUPPORT GROUPS PART OF YOUR LIFESTYLE
The first and second years in addiction recovery often include obstacles that seem so formidable you might be tempted to give up on the promise of healing altogether. You'll need the ongoing encouragement and support of others on the journey with you. If married, you should work toward your spouse becoming one of your key accountability partners.

ENLIST SPONSORS OR MENTORS
Your group leader, pastor, or counselor may be able to link you up with a sponsor or mentor who's already demonstrated steady progress in walking with God on the path to freedom, healing, and wholeness.

SEEK COUNSELING OR THERAPY GROUPS
Beyond unplugging from pornography, the emotional and spiritual issues that drive sexual addiction often require the guidance of a trained professional. Find a Christian counselor who really knows the field of sexual addiction. To locate a professional who can help in individual counseling or therapy groups, check these organization's Web sites:

- National Council on Sexual Addiction and Compulsivity: www.ncsac.org
- Center for Sexual Wholeness: www.sexualwholeness.com/csw
- American Association of Christian Counselors: www.aacc.net
- The National Association for Christian Recovery: www.nacronline.com

- Bethesda Workshops: www.bethesdaworkshops.org
- Faithful and True Ministries: www.faithfulandtrueministries,com
- L.I.F.E. Ministries: www.freedomeveryday.org
- National Coalition for the Protection of Children & Families: www.nationalcoalition.org

CONSIDER MEDICAL HELP AND TREATMENT PROGRAMS

Given the type of issues often associated with sexual addictions, related issues like depression, anxiety, attention deficit disorders, anger, and so forth are likely also present. If support meetings, counseling, and medical evaluation are not enough, outpatient and inpatient programs have been developed for sex addictions. Bethesda Workshops are an excellent option for sex addicts, spouses, and couples (www.bethesdaworkshops.org).

For more detailed information on treatment approaches, read the book, *Healing the Wounds of Sexual Addiction* by Mark Laaser (Zondervan, 2004)

GROUP NEXT STEPS

At the end of this *Secret Seductress* experience, group members will feel a close sense of connection. At the same time, they 're aware that this is the final session. Depending upon your own plans for the group and/or the group views about continuing to meet and study another series, you need to be sensitive to what degree and sense of closure the group needs. Choose one or more of the following options ...

OPTION 1: Suggest to the group that redemptive community has had time to take root in your meetings together. Remind them that their healing journeys are only begin- ning. Ask the group if they would consider staying together for continued support and redemption. Pass around 3 x 5" cards so people can jot down their potential interest. Other related recovery studies in the Picking Up the Pieces series include *Stop the Madness* (addictions) and *Radical Reconciliation* (forgiveness). Consider also *Finding Jesus in the Movies*.

OPTION 2: Encourage group members to join the next *Secret Seductress* group, either to go through the process again at a deeper level, or to take to an active role in helping to lead the group as a mentor, small-group facilitator, accountability partner, or some other job that fits well. (As the group facilitator, try to fit people into the most suitable roles).

OPTION 3: If there are not enough to form a small group, refer these interested people to your pastor to connect them with an ongoing group. If you form a group that does not want to go through *The Secret Seductress* again, we suggest your next step would be to go through the Serendipity House study entitled *Great Beginnings*. You may order this and other group resources online at www.SerendipityHouse.com.

OPTION 4: Some support groups like to meet each month or so for a get-together at a restaurant. You may consider offering that as a recommendation. Knowing that a reunion is not far off may help many group members with this study's wrap-up, especially if you don't plan to continue meeting as a group.

MY PRAYER AND REQUESTS AND NEEDS:

MY GROUP'S PRAYER AND REQUESTS AND NEEDS:

TAKING IT HOME

A QUESTION TO TAKE TO YOUR HEART

※ If money was no object, what would you like to do that would make you come alive? If you were going to live out of your true glory and new name from the mouth of the Lord (Isaiah 62:2), what would your life look like?

CREATING A VISION

We encourage you to create your own Vision and Mission Statements. To help you with instructions in how to approach this important activity and in what to include, check out the article: "Creating a Vision for Your Adventure" at www.SerendipityHouse.com/Community/GroupMember.aspx soon.

1 John Piper, *What Jesus Demands from the World* (Wheaton, IL: Crossway Books, 2006.)

Group Meeting Structure

Each of your group meetings will include a four-part agenda.

1. Breaking the Ice:

This section includes fun, uplifting questions to warm up the group and help group members get to know one another better, as they begin the journey of becoming a connected community. These questions prepare the group for meaningful discussion throughout the session.

2. Discovering the Truth:

The heart of each session is the interactive Bible study time. The goal is for the group to discover biblical truths through open, discovery questions that lead to further investigation. The emphasis in this section is two-fold: (1) to provide instruction about the process of recovery and freedom; and (2) understand what the Bible says through interaction within your group.

NOTE: To help the group experience a greater sense of community, it is important for everybody to participate in the "Discovering the Truth" and "Embracing the Truth" discussions. Even though people in a group have differing levels of biblical knowledge, it is vital that group members encourage one another share what they are observing, thinking, and feeling about the Bible passages.

3. Embracing the Truth:

All study should direct group members to action and life change. This section continues the Bible study time, but with an emphasis on leading group members toward integrating the truths they have discovered into their lives. The questions are very practical and application-focused.

4. Connecting:

One of the key goals of this study is to lead group members to grow closer to one another as the group develops a sense of community. This section focuses on further application, as well as opportunities for encouraging, supporting, and praying for one another.

Taking it Home:

Between each session, there is some homework for group members. This includes a question to take to God or a question to take to the heart, and typically a few questions to help prepare for the next session. **These experiences are a critical part of your journey of healing and freedom.**

REQUIRED SUPPLIES AND PREPARATION
FOR EACH SESSION

This section lists the supplies required for the Group Experiences in each session of the study. The procedural instructions for the experiences are also given within each session.

SESSION 1:

Supplies: - 3x5 index cards and pens for each group member
- DVD player or Video cassette player
- DVD of the Lord of the rings movie, *The Two Towers*

Three Truths and a Lie Procedure:

Give each person a 3x5 card or a small sheet of paper and a pen. Read together the following writing instructions included in the session. After allowing a couple of minutes to write, go around the group and ask each person to share his four statements. Then have the group try to guess which of the statements was the lie. Acknowledge the person who is the best at identifying lies. After everyone has a turn, discuss the related questions.

Voices of Deception Procedure:

Read the introduction in the session to the group, and then show the clip from the second Lord of the Rings film, *The Two Towers*. On DVD-2, show Chapter 29 from the Special Extended Edition (1:38:35 to 1:41:05 minutes on the DVD timer) entitled "Gollum and Sméagol." On the Standard DVD Version, it's Chapter 22. After showing the clip, discuss the associated questions.

SESSION 2:

Supplies: - Audio CD player
- CD *Somebody's Daughter* available from Serendipity House

Is It Me? Procedure:

Page 4 shows a companion music CD called *Somebody's Daughter* available from Serendipity House. Have a CD player queued up to play the song "Is It Me?" from that CD. If you like, download lyrics from www.SerendipityHouse.com/Community (under Group Leaders - Leadership Aids). Ask group members to close their eyes and listen. Give a few moments for personal reflection at the end of the song and discuss the questions.

SESSION 3:

Supplies: - Four blindfolds
- 24 salted crackers (6 per team)
- Team 1: Cup of fresh, cold water
- Team 2: Sport drink such as Gatorade®
- Audio CD player
- CD *Somebody's Daughter* available from Serendipity House
- Team 3: Cold, carbonated cola
- Team 4: Cup of salt water
- A prize for the winning team
- Paper towels for cleaning up

Crunch & Chug Competition Procedure:
Set up a competition between four two-person teams. One member of each team will be the Feeder and the other will be the Cruncher/Chugger. Each Cruncher/Chugger will be blindfolded and sitting with hands behind his backs. At the start signal, each Feeder will stuff six crackers into the mouth of his blindfolded partner. Once the crackers are consumed, the Feeder will hold the cup as his partner chugs the drink. The first team to consume both crackers and drink is declared the winner. Award a prize, then discuss the related group questions.

Into the Light Procedure:
Page 4 shows a companion music CD called *Somebody's Daughter* available from Serendipity House. Have a CD player queued to play "Into the Light?" from that CD. If you like, you can download lyrics from www.SerendipityHouse.com/Community (under Group Leaders - Leadership Aids). Ask group members to close their eyes and listen with their hearts open. At the end of the song, discuss what each one heard using the related questions.

SESSION 4:

Supplies: - DVD player or Video cassette player
- DVD of the film *Gladiator*
- CD *Pursued by God: Redemptive Worship* by Serendipity House
- Pens or pencils

Survival Procedure:
Read the introduction to the group, then play a clip from the DreamWorks™ film *Gladiator*, starring Russell Crowe as Maximus. Show the core of Chapter 15, "The Battle of Carthage" (1:23:45 to 1:28:25 minutes on the Standard DVD timer; 1:30:40 to 1:34:16 minutes on the Extended Edition DVD). Note: Gladiator contains scenes with intense, graphic violence. After showing the clip, discuss the following questions.

Heart Writing Procedure:
Encourage the men to make the most of this exercise by being as honest as possible with themselves and with God.
1. Allow this experience some time; don't rush it.
2. Put on quiet background music (You may purchase the CD *Pursued by God: Redemptive Worship* from Serendipity House, or select your own music.)
3. Help each person create his own personal space. This is not a time to chat; make it very honoring.
4. Trust God to speak to each person individually through this exercise.
5. After allowing 10 minutes to write, invite group members to read their prayers aloud.

Instructions for Group Members: Take 10 minutes to write a brief prayer to God. Lead group members through the steps listed in the session.

SESSION 5:

Supplies: - Audio CD player
- CD *Somebody's Daughter* available from Serendipity House
- DVD player or Video cassette player
- DVD of the film *Saving Private Ryan*

Every Man's Battle Procedure:
Page 4 shows a companion music CD called *Somebody's Daughter* available from Serendipity House. Have a CD player queued up to play the song "Every Man's Battle—Remix" from that CD. If you like, you can download lyrics from www.SerendipityHouse.com/Community (under Group Leaders - Leadership Aids). Ask group members to close their eyes and listen with their hearts open. At the end of the song, discuss the associated questions.

Taking Thoughts Captive Procedure:
Read the introduction to the group, and then play a scene from the 1998 award-winning film *Saving Private Ryan*, starring Tom Hanks, Edward Burns, and Tom Sizemore. First, show the portion of Chapter 13, "Big Mystery" from 1:37:05 to 1:39:25 minutes on the DVD timer.

Next, show a second scene from *Saving Private Ryan*. Skip ahead to Chapter 18, "The Alamo." Show the very end of the scene beginning at 2:32:05 on the DVD timer. Continue into the beginning of Chapter 19, "The Bridge," and stop at the 2:35:05 mark. After showing the second scene, discuss the remaining questions

SESSION 6:

Supplies: - Chairs in a circle

Standing Together Procedure:
1. CIRCLE UP: Including yourself, divide the group in half (one half may have an extra person). Ask half the group to gather their seats in a circle and sit facing one another.

2. EXPLAIN: Each person standing needs to think of a short response to the following two statements. Read both statements aloud, then repeat them:
   "The root desire I believe I'm trying to fulfill with my secret seductress is _____ ,"
   "The most difficult thing for me about dumping my secret seductress is _____ ,"

3. SET UP: Give a minute or so for the standing people to think about their responses. Meanwhile, explain to the seated people that they should close their eyes and place both hands with palms up on the table or their laps. This signifies carrying the burdens of the people who speak from their hearts. Ask the standing people to gather around the outside of the circle, with one person standing behind each seated person.

4. EXPLAIN: Each person standing will lean down and share his responses in the right ear of the seated person. Then, each standing person will step to the right behind the next seated person and repeat those responses. Those standing will continue stepping to the right and speaking to each seated person until they're back where they started. REPEAT: Read the two statements again as review before the standing people begin.

5. GO: When everyone has some kind of response (it does not have to be earth-shaking), instruct the standing group to begin. When the circuit is completed, ask the people sitting to share any thoughts or feelings about what they heard. This is always amazingly insightful!

6. SWITCH: Ask the seated and standing people to switch positions. Repeat this exercise with the new standing group

Session 7:

OPTIONAL MOVIE NIGHT: Since *The Legend of Bagger Vance* plays such a central role in Session 7, we would encourage you to set up an additional meeting to watch the film together and be prepared to discuss it The one sexual situation is a good illustration of false intimacy.

Supplies: - DVD player or Video cassette player
         - DVD of the film *The Legend of Bagger Vance*

Back into the Shadows Procedure:
Read the introduction in the session aloud to the group, and then show a scene from the 2000 film, *The Legend of Bagger Vance*, starring Will Smith, Matt Damon, and Charlize Theron. Show part of Chapter 29 "The Drop" (begin about 4 minutes in at 1:37:08 and continue to end of Chapter 29 at 1:43:35 on the DVD timer). After showing the clip, discuss the following questions. *The Legend of Bagger Vance* is used as the basis for the rest of this session. Either pick key areas to discuss and keep things moving, or propose expanding this to cover two meetings.

Session 8:
Supplies: - Audio CD player
         - CD *Somebody's Daughter* available from Serendipity House

Lies of the Eyes Procedure:
Page 4 shows a companion music CD called *Somebody's Daughter* available from Serendipity House. Have a CD player queued up to play the poem "The Lies of the Eyes" from that CD. If you like, you can download lyrics from www.SerendipityHouse.com/Community (under Group Leaders - Leadership Aids). As group members listen, ask them to write down any thoughts or lines that affect them emotionally.

Lies of the Eyes Procedure:
Imagine you're observing your own funeral service. Your wife has the composure to make some remarks. One or more of your children want to speak. Other family and friends will share. Finally, God will sum up the substance and legacy of your life.

- What do I want my wife to be able to say? Write it here.
- What do I want my child(ren) to be able to say? Write it here.
- What do I want other family and friends to be able to say? Write it here.
- What would God say if my life continues down the path of sexual addiction? What do I want to hear Him say? Write it here.

LEADING A SUCCESSFUL RECOVERY GROUP

You need to accept the limitations of leadership. You cannot transform a life. You must lead your group to the Bible, the Holy Spirit, and the power of Christian community. By doing so your group will have all the tools necessary to walk through the healing journey and embrace life and hope on the other side. The journey must extend well beyond this study. But the experience will allow your group members to move toward wholeness.

Make the following things available at each session
- *The Secret Seductress* book for each attendee
- One copy for the group of the companion CD *Somebody's Daughter* (this powerful music and audio CD was designed to be used together for a recovery group *The Secret Seductress*)
- Bible for each attendee
- Boxes of tissue
- Snacks and refreshments plus dark chocolates (calming properties)
- Pens or pencils for each attendee

Every session requires other supplies for the group experiences that greatly enhance the healing journey. Check the supplies list and be sure you gather what's needed in each session.

The Setting

General Tips:

1. Prepare for each meeting by reviewing the material, praying for each group member, asking the Holy Spirit to join you, and making Jesus the centerpiece of every experience.

2. Create the right environment by making sure chairs are arranged so each person can see the eyes of every other attendee. Set the room temperature at 69 degrees. If meeting in a home, make sure pets are in a location where they cannot interrupt the meeting. Request that cell phones are turned off unless someone is expecting an emergency call. Have music playing as people arrive (volume low enough for people to converse) and, if possible, burn a sweet-smelling candle.

3. Try to have soft drinks and coffee available for early arrivals.

4. Have someone with the spiritual gift of hospitality ready to make any new attendees feel welcome.

5. Be sure there is adequate lighting so that everyone can read without straining.

6. There are four types of questions used in each session: Observation (What is the passage telling us?), Interpretation (What does the passage mean?), Self-revelation (How am I doing in light of the truth unveiled?), and Application (Now that I know what I know, what will I do to integrate this truth into my life?). You may not have time to use all the questions in each session, but be sure to use some from each of these types of questions.

7. Connect with group members away from group time. The amount of participation you'll receive from group member during meetings is directly related to the amount of time that you connect with them away from the meetings.

8. Don't get impatient about the depth of relationship group members are experiencing. Building real Christian Community takes time.

9. Be sure pens and/or pencils are available for attendees at each meeting.

10. Never ask someone to pray aloud without first getting their permission. Ask for volunteers to help with various aspects of the group, including reading aloud.

Every Meeting:

1. Before the icebreakers, do not say, "Now we're going to do an icebreaker." The meeting should feel like a conversation from beginning to end, not a classroom experience.

2. Be certain every member responds to the icebreaker questions. The goal is for every person to hear his own voice early in the meeting. People will then feel comfortable to converse later on. If group members can't think of a response, let them know you'll come back to them after the others have spoken.

3. Remember, a great group leader talks less than 10% of the time. If you ask a question and no one answers, just wait. If you create an environment where you fill the gaps of silence, the group will quickly learn they needn't join you in the conversation.

4. Don't be hesitant to call people by name as you ask them to respond to questions or to give their opinions. Be sensitive, but engage everyone in the conversation.

5. Don't ask people to read aloud unless you have gotten their permission prior to the meeting. Feel free to ask for volunteers to read.

The Group

Every group is made up of a unique set of personalities, backgrounds, and life experiences. This diversity creates a dynamic distinctivefor each group. Embracing the unique character of your group and its individuals is vital to a deep healing experience.

Treat each person as special, responsible, and valuable members of this Christian community. By doing so you'll bring out the best in each of them thus creating a living, breathing, life-changing group dynamic.

What Can You Expect?

Because group members are still experiencing and emotions are stirring within them, at the outset, members will be on their best behavior. Some attendees will, as they understand the openness necessary and requested by the group, withdraw for at time.

Some attendees will experience fatigue which will lead to them shutting down emotionally. This is natural and is one of the things our body does to prevent overload.

There are some emotions and phases unique to people dealing with sexual addictions. These will be addressed as the group progresses through the healing journey. Be sensitive.

You will be the most helpful when you focus on how each individual is adjusting and reminding them that hurt, anger , and other emotions are normal and extremely helpful to understand and express on the path to healing..

When short tempers, changes in physical habits, such as sleep, eating, apathy, and others appear to be long term, refer people to a pastor or competent Christian counselor. You can get a list of counselors from your pastor and through contacts provided in Session 8.

Places may also bring back memories or temptations that are difficult to deal with alone. If a member has an engagement in a location that would be a painful reminder of the past go with them and/or ask the group members if one of them might be there for this individual. You may hear, "This is something I have to do alone." You can respect this desire, but remind them that it's God who will give them strength, and that you will pray.

What Can You Do?

Support – Provide plenty of time for support among the group members. Encourage members to connect with each other between meetings. It's very important that you help each person in the group to develop a strong, supportive accountability group

Shared Feelings – Reassure the members how normal their feelings are; even if relief and sadness are mixed together. Encourage the members to share their feelings with one another.

Advice Giving – Encourage cross-talk (members talking to each other), but limit advice giving. "Should" and "ought to" statements tend to increase the guilt and shame.

Silence – Silence is not a problem. Even though it may seem awkward, silence is just a sign that people are not ready to talk. It DOES NOT mean they aren't thinking or feeling. If the silence needs to be broken, be sure you break it with the desire to move forward.

Prayer – Prayer is vital to healing. Starting and ending with prayer is important. However, people may need prayer in the middle of the session. If a member is sharing and you sense a need to pray, then begin to look for a place to add it.

Feelings vs. Right Choices and Thinking – There may be a temptation to overemphasize feelings rather that choices and thinking. It is important that you encourage the group to keep moving forward regardless of how we feel. Processing emotions is a vital aspect of the healing journey, but left to feelings alone, progress will shut down.

As you move toward the end of the study, be aware that it is a bittersweet time for the group. It will be painful for them to say goodbye to one another. Set a time for the group to have a reunion.

ABOUT THE AUTHORS

MARK LAASER is an internationally known author and speaker. His first book, *Healing the Wounds of Sexual Addiction*, was the first Christian book to address sexual addiction. He has since written more than six books including, *Talking to Your Kids About Sex* and *The Pornography Trap* (with Dr. Ralph Earle).

Dr. Laaser has ministered to hundreds of sex addicts and their families, consulted with churches, developed treatment programs for hospitals, and conducted seminars worldwide for 25 years.

He serves as director of the Institute for Healthy Sexuality of the American Association of Christian Counselors and as executive director of Faithful and True Ministries (www.faithfulandtrueministries.com). He's a member of the Society for the Advancement of Sexual Health and the National Association for Christian Recovery.

Dr. Laaser holds a PhD in Religion and Psychology from the Univ. of Iowa, and a Master of Divinity from Princeton Theological Seminary. He currently resides in Minnesota with his wife Debra. They have three grown children: Sarah, Jonathan, and Benjamin.

MICHAEL M. CHRISTIAN is a professional counselor in Nashville, Tennessee, focused on individual therapy, marital therapy, sex therapy, and treatment for sexual addiction. He also serves as a group therapist with Bethesda Workshops, a ministry that treats men and women who deal with sexual addiction and other sexual issues. His Web site is www.intimacyseekers.com.

Michael has earned both a Master of Divinity degree from The Southern Baptist Theological and a Master of Arts in Counseling from Trevecca Nazarene University (where he's also worked as an adjunct professor). Michael is a member of the American Association of Christian Counselors, American Association of Certified Christian Sexual Addiction Specialists, and American Association of Christian Sex Therapists. He is married for 28 years to his wife, Phyllis, and has one grown daughter, Rachel.

ACKNOWLEDGMENTS

This project was a true team effort. The authors wish to thank the team that labored so hard to make this life-changing small-group experience a reality.

- Publisher: Ron Keck
- Contributing Writers: Ben Colter (6 sessions) and Ramon Presson (2 sessions)
- Editorial team: Ben Colter, Karen Daniel, and Ron Keck
- Art direction and interior design: Scott Lee of Scott Lee Designs
- Cover design: Roy Roper of Wideyedesign

Special thanks to Zondervan for permission to draw extensively from Mark Laaser's book *Healing the Wounds of Sexual Addiction* © 1992, 1996, 2004.

GROUP DIRECTORY

Write your name on this page. Pass your books around and ask your group members to fill in their names and contact information in each other's books.

Your Name: _____

Name: _____ Name: _____
Address: _____ Address: _____
City: _____ City: _____
Zip Code: _____ Zip Code: _____
Home Phone: _____ Home Phone: _____
Mobile Phone: _____ Mobile Phone: _____
E-mail: _____ E-mail: _____

Name: _____ Name: _____
Address: _____ Address: _____
City: _____ City: _____
Zip Code: _____ Zip Code: _____
Home Phone: _____ Home Phone: _____
Mobile Phone: _____ Mobile Phone: _____
E-mail: _____ E-mail: _____

Name: _____ Name: _____
Address: _____ Address: _____
City: _____ City: _____
Zip Code: _____ Zip Code: _____
Home Phone: _____ Home Phone: _____
Mobile Phone: _____ Mobile Phone: _____
E-mail: _____ E-mail: _____

Name: _____ Name: _____
Address: _____ Address: _____
City: _____ City: _____
Zip Code: _____ Zip Code: _____
Home Phone: _____ Home Phone: _____
Mobile Phone: _____ Mobile Phone: _____
E-mail: _____ E-mail: _____

Name: _____ Name: _____
Address: _____ Address: _____
City: _____ City: _____
Zip Code: _____ Zip Code: _____
Home Phone: _____ Home Phone: _____
Mobile Phone: _____ Mobile Phone: _____
E-mail: _____ E-mail: _____